Why do Employees Leave an Organisation?

Almonds: Good for the Heart

ISSN 0

I0476120

Business and Economic

Facts

FOR YOU

Pages: 52

www.ffymag.com **AUGUST 2014**

An *EFY* GROUP Publication

Essential Traits of SUCCESSFUL BUSINESSWOMEN IN RURAL INDIA

Market Surveys

The Advantages of Aquaculture

Radish: Abundant Growth, Poor Marketing

Cement: Capacity Exceeds Consumption

Banking

Non-Performing Assets: Banks Must Spot the Early Warning Signs

The Challenges Posed by Frauds in the Banking Sector

Business and Economic Facts FOR YOU

Vol. 34   No. 11

ISSN-0970-2652

EDITOR : S.P. Chopra

EDITORIAL : Editorial Secretary
CORRESPONDENCE Phone: 011-26810601
E-mail: editsec@efy.in

SUBSCRIPTIONS & : Customer Care Officer, EFY
MISSING ISSUES Phone: 011-26810601 or 02 or 03
E-mail: support@efy.in

BACK ISSUES : Kits'n'Spares, New Delhi
Phone: 011-26371661, 26371662
E-mail: info@kitsnspares.com

EXCLUSIVE : IBH Books & Magazine Distributors Ltd, Mumbai
NEWSSTAND Phone: 022-40497401, 40497402, 40497474,
DISTRIBUTOR 40497413; Fax: 40497434
E-mail: circulations@ibhworld.com

ADVERTISEMENTS : Phone: 011-26810601 or 02 or 03
NEW DELHI Fax: 26817563
(HEAD OFFICE) E-mail: efyenq@efy.in

MUMBAI : Ph: 022-24950047, 24928520
E-mail: efymum@efy.in

BENGALURU : Ph: 080-25260394, 25260023
E-mail: efyblr@efy.in

CHENNAI : Ph: 09916390422
E-mail: efyenq@efy.in

HYDERABAD : Ph: 09916390422
E-mail: efyenq@efy.in

KOLKATA : Ph: 08800094202
E-mail: efyenq@efy.in

PUNE : Ph: 09223232006
E-mail: efypune@efy.in

GUJARAT : Ph: 09821267855
E-mail: cfyahd@efy.in

CHINA : Power Pioneer Group Inc.
Ph: (86 755) 83729797, (86) 13923802595
E-mail: powerpioneer@efy.in

JAPAN : Tandem Inc., Ph: 81-3-3541-4166
E-mail: tandem@efy.in

SINGAPORE : Publicitas Singapore Pte Ltd
Ph: +65-6836 2272
E-mail: publicitas@efy.in

TAIWAN : J.K. Media, Ph: 886-2-87726780 ext. 10
E-mail: jkmedia@efy.in

UNITED STATES : E & Tech Media
Ph: +1 860 536 6677
E-mail: veroniquelamarque@gmail.com

SUBSCRIPTION RATES

Period	Newsstand Price (₹)	Discounted Price (₹)
5 Years	6000	3590
3 Years	3600	2510
1 Year	1200	950

1. Includes delivery by ordinary post/courier.
2. Please add ₹ 50/- for outside-Delhi cheques.
3. All payments should be sent in favour of EFY Enterprises Pvt Ltd, D-87/1, Okhla Industrial Area, Phase-1, New Delhi 110020.
4. Do mention the name of the magazine required in your covering letter or money order coupon.
5. Non-receipt of copies may be reported to support@efy.in mentioning your subscription number.

CONTENTS

DEPARTMENTS

SOME FORTHCOMING EVENTS

July 31-August 3, 2014:
• The Finance, MIS, Economics & Global Business Research Conference, Istanbul, Turkey

August 1, 2014:
• National Case Study Conference, Bengaluru, Karnataka, India

August 1-3, 2014:
• Annual International Conference on Law, Economics and Politics (AICLEP 2014), Oxford, United Kingdom
• International Conference on Tourism Transport and Technology at the Brunel University, London, United Kingdom
• First Asia Pacific Conference on Global Business, Economics, Finance and Social Sciences, Singapore

August 2-3, 2014:
• International Conference on Advances in Economics, Management and Social Study - EMS 2014, Kuala Lumpur, Malaysia

August 3-4, 2014:
• 13th GABER International Conference, Istanbul, Turkey

August 3-7, 2014:
• The 2014 Clute Institute International Academic Conference, San Francisco, California, United States of America

August 4-5, 2014:
• Final Call For Papers: 9th Annual London Business Research Conference, London, United Kingdom
• Business and Social Science Research Conference: Dubrovnik 2014, Dubrovnik, Croatia (Hrvatska)

August 4-6, 2014:
• TCSSE International Conference of Social Science and Education, New York, United States of America

August 5-6, 2014:
• 2nd International Conference on New Directions in Business, Management, Finance and Economics (ICNDBM 2014), Tbilisi, Georgia

August 6-7, 2014:
• UGC-Sponsored International Seminar on "Women Entrepreneurship - A Global Perspective" (INSWEG-2014), Vijayawada, Andhra Pradesh, India

August 6-8, 2014:
• International Conference on Business, Information, and Cultural Creative Industry, Taipei, Taiwan
• 2014 2nd Journal Conference on Trade, Economics and Finance (JCTEF 2014 2nd), Singapore
• 4th Global Chinese Management Studies Conference (CMS 2014), Singapore

August 7-8, 2014:
• International Academic Conference on Economics, Management and Marketing in Prague 2014, Prague, Czech Republic
• International Conference on Management in 21st Century (ICM21), Tehran, Iran
• LCBR European Marketing Conference 2014, Munich, Bavaria, Germany

August 7-9, 2014:
• International Symposium on Finance, Insurance and Economics, Taipei, Taiwan

August 11-12, 2014:
• International Academic Conference in Paris, France

August 11-13, 2014:
• South Asian International Conference, Islamabad, Pakistan

August 12-15, 2014:
• Knowledge Management International Conference (KMIC), Langkawi, Kedah, Malaysia

August 13-15, 2014:
• Finance and Economics Conference 2014, Munich, Bavaria, Germany

August 17-20, 2014:
• SPEC 2014 Shedding New Light on Disease, Krakow, Poland

August 18-19, 2014:
• International SME Conference (ISMEC 2014), Kuala Lumpur, Malaysia

August 18-20, 2014:
• International Case Study Conference 2014, Kuala Lumpur, Malaysia
• International Conference on Accounting Studies (ICAS 2014), Kuala Lumpur, Malaysia

August 20-22, 2014:
• Cretech2014, Bangkok, Thailand

August 29-31, 2014:
• EUMMAS 2014 International Conference on Marketing, Management and Economics, Sarajevo, Bosnia and Herzegovina

September 1-3, 2014:
• Annual International Conference on Law, Economics and Politics (AICLEP 2014), Oxford, United Kingdom

September 1-4, 2014:
• Prague 12th International Academic Conference - The IISES, Prague, Czech Republic

September 1-5, 2014:
• Economy and Business 2014, 13th International Conference, Elenite Holiday Village, Burgas, Bulgaria

September 2-3, 2014:
• 5th International Conference on E-business, Management and Economics - ICEME 2014, Kuala Lumpur, Malaysia

September 17, 2014:
• Strategic Business, Management, and Economic Research International Conference, Washington DC, United States of America

September 17-19, 2014:
• Business Management Conference (BMC2014), Durban, KwaZulu-Natal, South Africa

September 21-24, 2014:
• First International Conference on Genomics, Traits and Business, Charlotte, North Carolina, United States of America

September 22-23, 2014:
• The Arab Women in Leadership and Business Summit, Dubai, United Arab Emirates

September 26-27, 2014:
• The 3rd International Conference on Wireless Networks (ICWN 2014), Bali, Indonesia

October 1-2, 2014:
• International Conference on Business, Law and Corporate Social Responsibility (ICBLCSR'14), Phuket, Thailand

October 6-8, 2014:
• The Third International Conference on Informatics & Applications (ICIA 2014), Kuala Terengganu, Malaysia

October 7-10, 2014:
• Second Annual International Symposium on Comparative Sciences, Sofia, Bulgaria

October 13-14, 2014:
• 2nd International Conference on e-Business and e-Commerce Management - ICBCM 2014, Tbilisi, Georgia

October 15-17, 2014:
• EABTH2014 European Academic Conference on Business Tourism and Hospitality, Toronto, Ontario, Canada

October 28, 2014:
• 4th Asia eCommerce Conference 2014, Kuala Lumpur, Wilayah Persekutuan, Malaysia

November 27-30, 2014:
• 12th International Conference on Knowledge, Economy and Management, Antalya, Turkey

(Source: Conal Conference Alerts)

THE LAST ISSUE!

What you are holding in your hands is the last issue of Facts For You magazine. With a sad heart, we are closing down this publication due to several reasons.

Facts For You started as a bi-monthly magazine in July 1979. Since then it changed many ways in content, periodicity and looks, besides its price. As it was being published without any advertisement support since a long time, it was becoming increasingly difficult to continue due to the rising costs.

Fortunately, with the advent of the Internet and search engines like Google, you will now be able to access most of the information online in digital form. But when Facts For You was launched, such information could only be made available in print.

Over the years we continued publishing Facts For You, in spite of rising costs, because of many reasons. One of them was that, the magazine was educative not only for the readers but also for us, the editors and the publishers. We loved producing it.

But everything has a time line. And that time line has come for Facts For You. So, with a heavy heart, we bid adieu to the readers and the contributors to the magazine! Arrangements are being made to refund the non-used part of the money received for subscriptions to all concerned.

Thanks for your support all these years!

NATIONAL HEALTH MISSION EXPENDITURES, 2007-2014

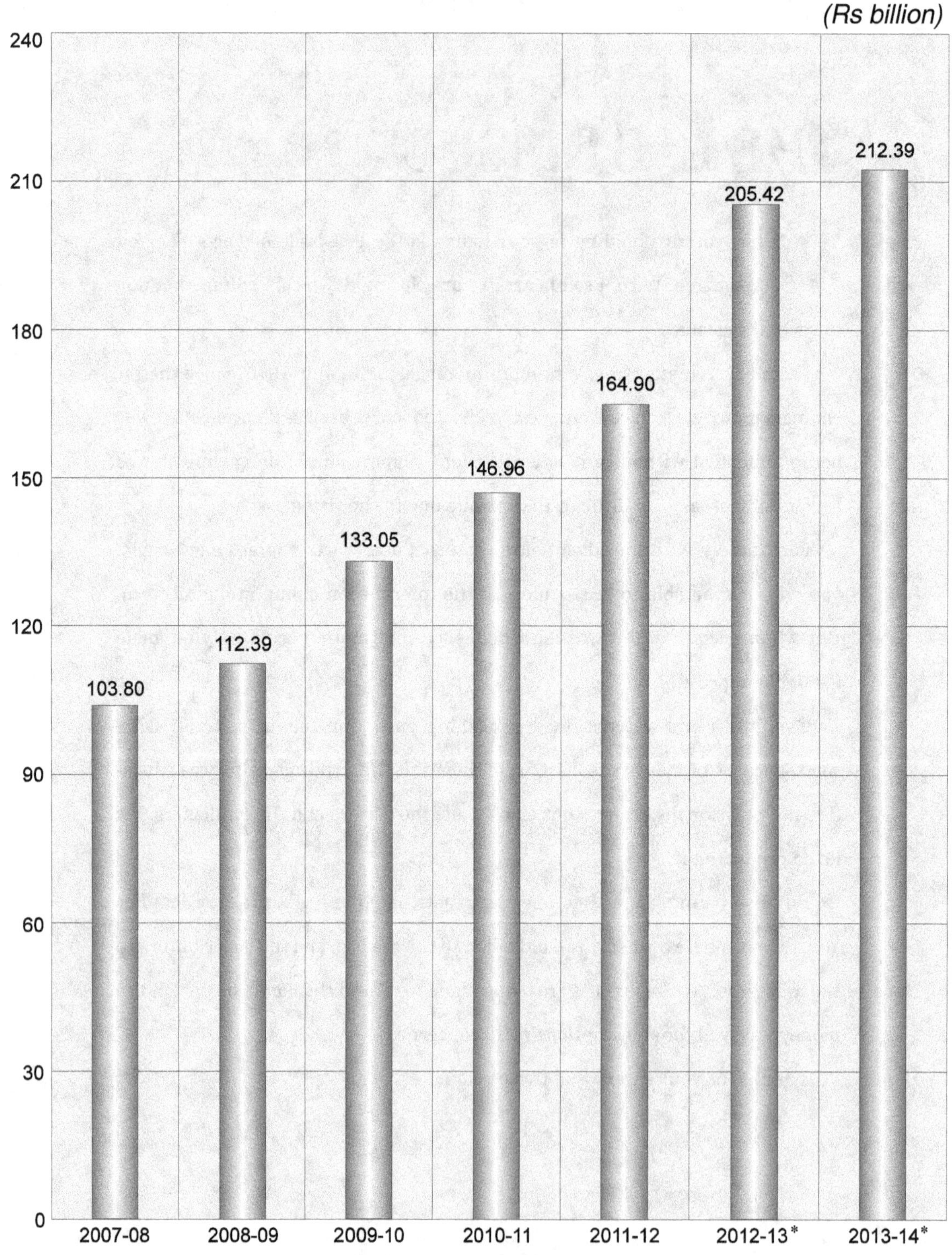

(Rs billion)

240

210

180

150

120

90

60

30

0

| 2007-08 | 2008-09 | 2009-10 | 2010-11 | 2011-12 | 2012-13* | 2013-14* |

Bar values: 103.80, 112.39, 133.05, 146.96, 164.90, 205.42, 212.39

*Budget estimates
Source: NRHM & Union Budget

FIXED-DEPOSIT INTEREST RATES OF SOME REPUTED BANKS

(for amounts below ₹ 10 million, as on July 30, 2014)

Name of the Bank	Interest for			Period for maximum interest	Maximum interest offered
	Min. period (7-14 days)	One year	Three years		
	General	General	General		General
Allahabad Bank	5.00%	9.05%	9.05%	1 year to less than 5 years	9.05%
Andhra Bank	6.00%	9.00%	8.75%	444 days	9.05%
Bank of Baroda	4.50%	9.05%	9.05%	1 year to 10 years	9.05%
Bank of Maharashtra	6.50%	9.00%	8.75%	181 days to 365 days	9.00%
Canara Bank	4.00%	9.05%	9.05%	1 year to 10 years	9.05%
Central Bank of India	6.50%	9.00%	9.05%	777 days	9.15%
Citibank	3.00%	7.50%	6.75%	365-400 days	7.00%
ICICI Bank	4.50%	8.00%	8.75%	390 days to 2 years	9.00%
IDBI Bank	6.00% (15 days-45 days)	9.10%	9.00%	500 days	9.30%
Oriental Bank of Commerce	4.00%	9.00%	8.75%	1 year to less than 3 years	9.00%
Punjab National Bank	4.00%	9.00%	9.00%	1 year to 10 years	9.00%
Punjab & Sind Bank (Amount between ₹ 100,000 and ₹ 10 mn)	4.00%	9.15%	9.00%	1 year to 5 years	9.15%
South Indian Bank	4.00% (15 days-45 days)	9.00%	8.75%	400 days	9.00%
State Bank of India	7.00% (7 days-179 days)	9.00%	8.75%	1 year to less than 3 years	9.00%
Syndicate Bank	7.10%	9.11%	8.50%	One year exact	9.11%
UCO Bank	7.50%	9.10%	9.00%	One year exact	9.10%

Source: Bank websites (Please re-confirm the latest rates before investing)

BY: DR A. SUJATHA

TRAITS OF SUCCESSFUL WOMEN ENTREPRENEURS IN RURAL INDIA

Rural self-employment of women has a crucial role to play in the context of the high unemployment rate in rural India, which leads to the migration of labour from rural to urban centres. This article explores the traits women must have in order to successfully run their own units in rural India.

The economy of rural India remains stagnant. Most of the rural population comprises agricultural labourers who get employment only during particular seasons. A major percentage of agriculturists hold less than one hectare of land. Productivity in agriculture is still low and most of the small farmers are in a vicious circle of poverty. So agriculture itself is not in a position to provide full employment in rural areas. Unemployment in rural areas is steadily increasing, driving the migration from rural to urban areas.

In India, women constitute 48 per cent of the total population, 60 per cent of the rural unemployed and 56 per cent of the total employed population. A substantial number of women are unemployed but have the ability to undertake industrial activity. In this context, it is essential to develop women's entrepreneurship qualities in order to expose them to various profit generating avenues. And in some parts of our country, women have proved their talents as successful entrepreneurs.

Entrepreneurial talents exist in every person, though in varying degrees. Many attempts have been made to identify the unique traits associated with entrepreneurial suc-

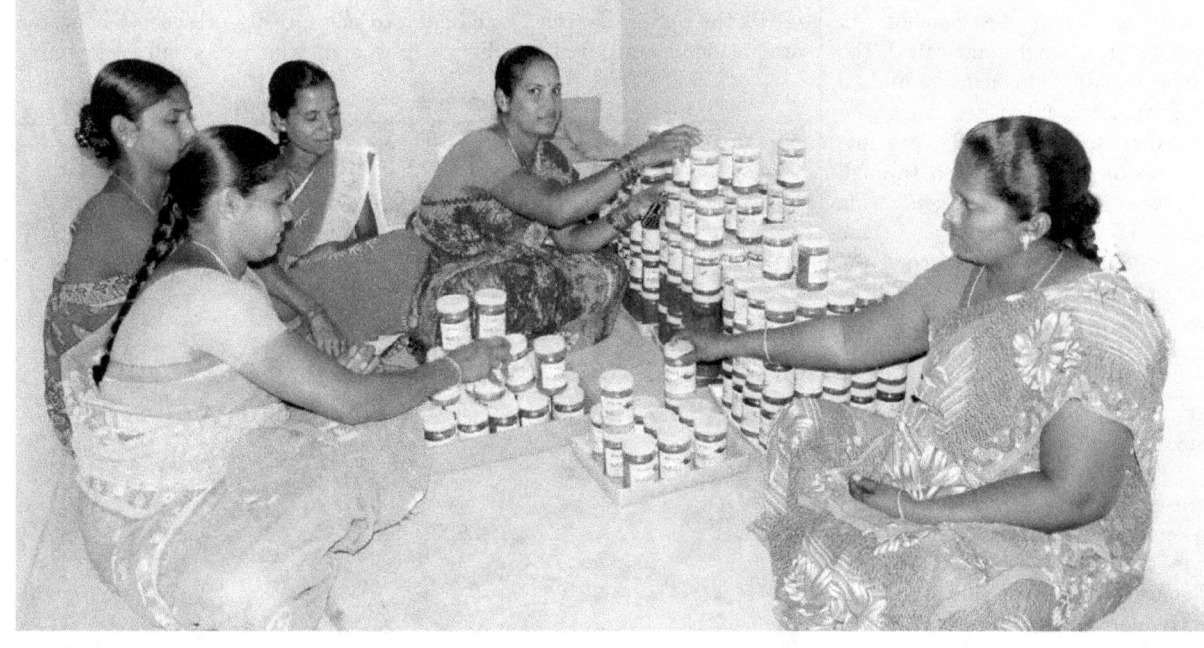

Table I
Self-confidence

Variables	Mean	SD	CV	Rank	SK
Capable of achieving goals	4.72	0.4497	9.52	I	0.985
Positive attributes	4.28	0.6023	14.07	IV	-0.211
Aware of strengths and weaknesses	4.44	0.6692	15.07	V	-1.194
Trust in one's own judgement	4.36	0.5208	11.94	III	-0.152
Ventures forth with self-confidence	4.40	0.4907	11.15	II	-0.410

Source: Computed data

cess. However, these traits do not seem to be universal. Cultural and other factors appear to be important. Therefore, one does not become a successful entrepreneur by the mere act of starting an enterprise.

The problem

India is a developing country and has been facing an acute and chronic unemployment problem. Hence, the tremendous entrepreneurial talent of women has to be properly harnessed, resulting in their fruitful employment and their contributing to the nation's social and economic development. Various pilot programmes have been launched by the government to encourage and accelerate rural development. In particular, a programme called 'Development of Women and Children in Rural Areas (DWCRA)' was introduced as far back as 1982 to promote the status of rural women through the creation of income generating activities. However, many of these programmes have not reached the target groups, namely, the potential women entrepreneurs, on time and have not empowered them. One of the main reasons for such a state of affairs is the high rate of illiteracy among women.

Though women have indeed progressed, their development has not been sufficient. Hence, there is a need to evaluate the factors that influence entrepreneurship in order to introduce the right measures for the further development of women-led businesses.

In a study conducted on women entrepreneurs in the Theni district of Tamil Nadu, the author collected primary data by way of well-structured interviews. And the required secondary data was collected from the government agencies, books, magazines, journals, bulletins and periodicals.

There are thirty districts in Tamil Nadu. By bifurcating the erstwhile Madurai district, the government formed Theni district in 1997. The district has five taluks, namely Bodinayakanur, Aundipatti, Periyakulam, Theni and Uttamapalayam. As per the data available with the District Industries Centre (DIC), the sample district Theni had around 3419 registered small scale

industrial units as on 31.03.2005, of which 342 small-scale units were run by women, of which 37 units were defunct. Five women entrepreneurs were reluctant to part with information about their units. The remaining 300 units were selected for this study.

Assessment of entrepreneurial traits

Self-confidence. Women entrepreneurs need the ability to stick to their goals through thick and thin and not get disheartened by setbacks. An entrepreneur must have the mental capacity to face any situation and also have the ability to inspire others. She must have the confidence in herself and the determination to achieve her goals. She must be aware of her strengths and weaknesses. Positive thinking and an optimistic approach creates a favourable atmosphere to get things done. She must have strong faith in her own abilities and she must stick to her own judgments in the face of opposition. As sustained self-confidence is an important trait for any entrepreneur, an attempt was made to measure its presence among the women who ran small scale units,

considering five variables as presented in Table I.

Table I shows that the co-efficient of variations (CV) is the least for the variable 'Capable of achieving goals', followed by the variables 'Ventures forth with self-confidence', 'Trust in one's own judgement', 'Positive attributes' and 'Awareness about strengths and weaknesses', respectively. Table I also shows that these five variables are found to be negatively skewed and, hence, it may be concluded that a majority of the respondents possess all these attributes.

Risk taking and problem solving. Women entrepreneurs should be capable of taking calculated risks but should not speculate or gamble. They should be able to study the market situation, explore profitability in different lines of business, evaluate products, machinery and finance options, before taking a final decision. But women who have typically been protected by male members of the family rarely have these abilities.

A successful entrepreneur invariably is a risk taker when compared to others. Women entrepreneurs who operate ventures in rural areas normally take low or moderate risks with a fairly reasonable chance of achieving their objectives. As continuous risk taking and problem solving is an important aspect of entrepreneurship, an attempt was made to evaluate this trait among women business owners. Five variables were considered, as presented in Table II.

Table II shows that the co-efficient of variation is the least for the variable 'Courage to face the unknown', followed by the variables 'Alternative strategies considered', 'A strong belief in luck', 'Taking decisions even if not sure of the outcome' and 'Capable of taking risks in relationships' . The table also shows that all these five variables are found to be negatively skewed and, hence, it may be concluded that a majority

Table II
Risk Taking and Problem Solving

Variable	Mean	SD	CV	Rank	SK
Takes decisions even if not sure of the outcome	4.1600	0.9258	22.8	IV	−0.934
Capable of taking risks in relationships	4.1400	0.9398	23.9	V	−1.01
Courage to face the unknown	4.3800	0.4862	11.0	I	0.497
Considers alternative strategies	4.4800	0.5004	11.16	II	0.080
A strong belief in luck	3.6000	0.6644	18.4	III	0.661

Source: Computed data

Table III
Leadership and Motivation

Variable	Mean	SD	CV	Rank	SK
Capable of motivating others	3.6200	0.6300	17.4	IV	0.508
Participates in union/club related activities	3.2600	0.4393	13.4	III	1.10
Accepts leadership roles	4.3000	0.4590	10.67	I	0.877
Makes an effort to encourage others	4.5400	0.4992	11.61	II	−0.161
Represents problems to authorities	2.6600	0.4745	17.83	V	−0.679

Source: Computed data

of the respondents possess all these attributes.

Leadership and motivation. Entrepreneurs are not motivated by profit alone. There are a number of other factors such as educational background, occupational experience, desire to work independently, family background, assistance from government and financial institutions, availability of raw materials, etc, which inspire entrepreneurs.

In order to achieve the goals, co-operative efforts from others are indispensable. Winning the confidence and recognition of others is also considered to be a pre-requisite for successful entrepreneurship.

As 'persistent leadership with a sense of motivation' is an important trait of entrepreneurial skill, an attempt was made to measure the degree of its presence among the women in the study, for which five variables were considered as presented in Table III.

Table III shows that the co-efficient of variation is the least for the variable 'Accepts leadership roles', followed by the other variables. The table also shows that all these five variables are found to be negatively skewed and, hence, it may be concluded that a majority of the respondents possess all these attributes.

Innovation and initiative. The ability to spot and seize opportunities results in a fair chance of success. An innovative bent of mind that is ingrained right from childhood, coupled with the enterprise to turn difficulties into opportunities, will help women take the right path. They have to be realistic in choosing from their options, and be prepared to keep their personal likes and dislikes aside in order to achieve their goals. An emotional attitude towards solving problems that they may encounter from time to time is generally considered to be a stumbling block to progress. Those who conceptualise new ideas and are prepared to try out alternatives within no time, when something goes wrong, will definitely come out with flying

colours. Similarly, a willingness to avail the services of innovative thinkers will add a winning ingredient to any endeavour.

Decision-making. Running a business requires taking a number of decisions. Hence, an entrepreneur should have the capacity to analyse various aspects of the business prior to arriving at a decision. A successful entrepreneur approaches her business problems with an open mind and, normally, is not rigid. In other words, she does not hesitate to revise her decisions if something goes wrong. Keeping the problems pending in business affairs can prove costly and, hence, quick and prompt decisions will always be appreciated.

Human relations. The most important entrepreneurial traits that contribute to the success of an enterprise are emotional stability, personal relations, consideration and tactfuless. In other words, maintenance of inter-personal relations often makes the difference between success and failure. An entrepreneur is expected to have cordial relationships with her customers in order to gain their continued patronage and to win their confidence. She must also maintain good relations with her employees if she wishes to motivate them to higher levels of efficiency. An entrepreneur who maintains harmonious relations with customers, employees, suppliers and creditors is more likely to succeed in her endeavors.

Some recommendations

1. In order to motivate women to participate in enterprise-building, the government could periodically select successful business ventures and successful women entrepreneurs in every district and honour them with awards.

2. Business training can be imparted to women entrepreneurs frequently by the government with the assistance of non-government organisations.

3. A 'Government—Entrepreneurs Association' could be formed to offer counselling and to provide consultancy services to solve the problems faced by women entrepreneurs.

Self-employment becomes significant in India owing to the growing unemployment problem. Over population has made it virtually impossible for the government and the private sector to provide employment opportunities for all. The pressure of unemployment has increased with more women in search of employment opportunities. Self-employment can also provide a greater degree of independence to women and offers them scope for innovation. It is a test of one's own talents and capabilities. ■

The author heads the PG Department of Commerce (CA) at Sri Kaliswari College in Sivakasi, Tamil Nadu

BY: K. SIVA SANKAR
G. RAMESH PANDI

MANAGEMENT OF NON-PERFORMING ASSETS: THE CHALLENGES FACED BY INDIAN BANKS

Non-performing assets are a drag on the profitability of any bank. It is important that banks build early warning signals into their operations, so that potential loan defaulters are spotted before they can cause undue harm to the financial institution.

The term Non-Performing Assets (NPAs) refers to an advance facility, in respect of which the interest or instalment of principal has remained overdue for a period exceeding 90 consecutive days. An asset becomes non-performing when it ceases to generate income for the bank. The guiding principle is that the income on NPAs should not be recognised on accrual basis and should be treated as income only when actually received. Moreover, banks have been instructed that the interest on NPAs should not be taken as the income.

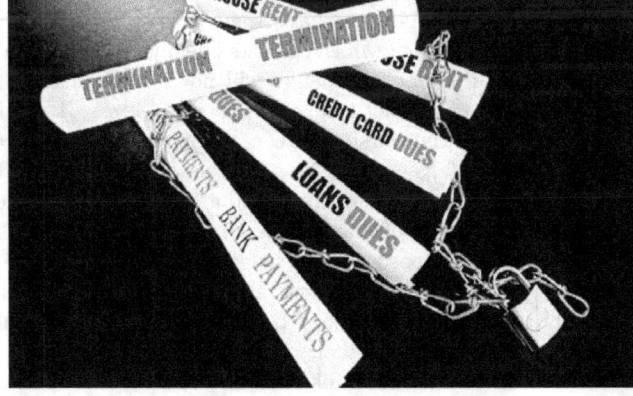

Common classification of assets

Once an asset falls under the NPA category, banks are required by the Reserve Bank of India (RBI) to make provision for the uncollected interest on these assets. For this purpose they have to classify their assets, based on the strength and on collateral securities, into four types, as mentioned below:

Standard assets. A standard asset is an asset that does not pose any problem—it is not a non-performing asset. Since this asset does not carry any extra risk, banks were not required to make any provision for uncollected interest for these assets in the past. At present, however, they need to keep a small provision of 0.25 per cent of total outstandings.

Sub-standard assets. A sub-standard asset is an asset that has been a NPA for a period not exceeding two years. A general provision of 10 per cent of total outstandings should be made in this category.

Doubtful assets. A doubtful asset was earlier an asset that had been a NPA for a period exceeding two years. This period was reduced to 18 months with effect from March 31, 2001. The general provision to be made on this asset is: up to one year—20 per cent; one year to three years—30 per cent; and more than 3 years—50 per cent.

Loss assets. A loss asset is an asset that has been identified by the banks, the internal or external auditors, or the RBI inspectors, but the amount has not been written off fully or partly.

Even though accounts are classified as standard, sub-standard, doubtful and loss assets, if these are not realisable, such advances can be straightaway classified as NPAs, irrespective of the stipulated period mentioned by the bank authorities.

Guidelines for minimising NPAs

Banks are required to follow certain guidelines in order to minimise the non-performing assets. These are listed below:

Use of appropriate internal systems. Banks should establish appropriate internal systems to eliminate delays or postponement in the identification of NPAs, especially for high value accounts.

Classification of accounts with temporary deficiencies. The classification of an asset as a NPA should be based on the record of recovery. Banks should not classify an advance account as an NPA merely due to the existence of some deficiencies, which are temporary in nature, such as non-availability of adequate drawing power based on latest stock.

Asset classification should be borrower-wise and not facility-wise. It is difficult to envisage a situation where only one asset of a borrower becomes a problem with respect to recovery. Therefore, all the assets loaned by a bank to a borrower have to be treated as NPAs, and not a particular asset or a part thereof, interest payment for which has become irregular.

Advances under consortium arrangements. Asset classification of advances taken from consortiums should be based on the record of recovery of the individual member banks, as well as other aspects that have a bearing on the recoverability of these advances.

Agricultural advances. (a) In respect of advances granted for agricultural purposes, if the interest or instalment of principal remains unpaid for two harvest seasons after it becomes due, this advance is to be treated as a NPA.

(b) When natural calamities impair the repaying capacity of agricultural borrowers, banks may convert a short-term production loan into a term loan, or re-schedule the repayment period as a relief measure. In this case, the term loan as well as fresh short-term loan may be treated as current dues and need not be classified as a NPA.

Restructuring/rescheduling of loans. A standard asset, where the terms of the loan arrangement regarding interest and principal have been renegotiated or rescheduled after the commencement of production, should be treated as a sub-standard asset and should remain in that category for at least one year of satisfactory performance under the renegotiated or restructured terms. In case of sub-standard and doubtful assets also, rescheduling does not entitle a bank to upgrade the quality of advances automatically, unless there is satisfactory performance under the rescheduled/renegotiated terms.

The financial impact of NPAs

The failure of banks to recover interest and principal payments from NPAs could have some disastrous effects, which are listed below:

1. Owners of banks will not receive a market return on their capital. In the worst case scenario, if the bank fails, owners lose their assets. In modern times, this could affect a broad pool of shareholders.

2. Depositors will not receive a market return on savings. In the worst case scenario, if the bank fails, depositors lose their assets or uninsured balance. Banks will also redistribute losses to other borrowers by charging higher interest rates. Lower deposit rates and higher lending rates repress savings and financial markets, which hampers economic growth.

3. Non-performing loans represent bad investments. NPAs misallocate credit from good projects, which do not receive funding, to failed projects. Bad investments end up in misallocation of capital and, by extension, labour and natural resources. The economy performs below its production potential.

4. Non-performing loans may spill over the banking system and contract the money stock, which may lead to a financial crisis. This can happen if:

(i) Many borrowers fail to pay interest and banks begin to experience liquidity shortages. These shortages can jam payments across the country.

(ii) Due to illiquidity, banks are unable to pay depositors—for example, cash their pay cheques. This will lead to financial panic.

(iii) Under-capitalised banks exceed the bank's capital base.

The main underlying reasons for NPAs in India

An internal study conducted by the RBI shows that the following factors, in order of importance, contribute to NPAs:

1. Diversion of funds for expansion/modernisation
2. Taking up of new projects
3. Helping/promoting associate concerns
4. Business (product, marketing, etc) failure
5. Inefficiency in management
6. Slackness in credit management and monitoring
7. Use of inappropriate technology/technical problems
8. Lack of co-ordination among lenders
9. External factors
10. General recession
11. Input/power shortage
12. Price escalation
13. Exchange rate fluctuations
14. Accidents and natural calamities, etc.
15. Changes in government policies in excise/import duties, pollution control orders, etc.

Financial sector experts offer a few other reasons for NPAs in India.

These are listed below.

Liberalisation of the economy. The liberalisation of the Indian economy led to the removal of foreign trade restrictions and a reduction in import tariffs. A large number of borrowers were unable to compete in a free market, in which lower prices and greater choices were available to consumers. Further, borrowers operating in specific industries suffered due to political, fiscal and social compulsions that resulted from liberalisation (e.g., sugar and fertiliser industries).

Tax monitoring of credits. Loan proposals generally pass through many levels of scrutiny before approval is granted. However, the monitoring of sometimes-complex credit files has not received the attention it needed, which meant that early warning signals were not recognised and standard assets slipped to the NPA category without banks being able to take proactive measures to prevent this from happening. Adverse trends in borrowers' performance were not noted in time.

Over-optimistic promoters. Promoters were often optimistic with respect to setting up of large projects and, in some cases, their intentions were not above board. Screening procedures did not always highlight these issues. Often, projects were set up with the expectation that part of the funding would be arranged from the capital markets, which were booming at the time of the project appraisal. When the capital markets subsequently crashed, the requisite funds could never be raised, promoters often lost interest and lenders were left stranded with incomplete or unviable projects.

Directed lending. Loans to some segments were dictated by government policies rather than commercial imperatives.

Highly leveraged borrowers. Some borrowers were under capitalised and over burdened with debt to absorb the changing economic situation in the country. Operating within a protected market resulted in low appreciation of commercial/market risk.

Funding mismatch. In many cases, loans granted for the short term were used to fund long-term transactions.

High cost of funds. Interest rates as high as 20 per cent were not uncommon. Borrowers could not service this high-cost debt.

Willful defaulters. There were a number of borrowers who strategically defaulted on their debt service obligations, as they realised that the legal recourse available to creditors was slow in achieving results.

Procedures for NPA identification and resolution in India

Since a high number of NPAs dampens the performance of banks, it is important to identify potential problem accounts and monitor them closely. Though most banks have Early Warning Systems (EWS) for identification of potential NPAs, the actual processes followed differ from bank to bank. The EWS enables a bank to identify the borrower accounts that show signs of credit deterioration and initiate remedial action. Many banks have evolved and adopted an elaborate EWS, which allows them to identify potential distress signals and plan their options beforehand, accordingly.

The early warning signals indicate potential problems in the accounts, which include persistent irregularity in accounts and delays in servicing of interest payments. In addition, some of these banks review their exposure to borrower accounts every quarter based on published data, which serves as an important additional warning system. These early warning signals used by banks are generally independent of the risk rating systems and asset classification norms prescribed by RBI.

The major components or processes of the EWS followed by banks in India, as brought out by a study conducted by Reserve Bank of India at the insistence of the Board of Financial Supervision, are as follows:

1. Appointing a relationship manager/credit officer for monitoring accounts

2. Preparation of 'know your client' profiles

3. Following a credit rating system

4. Identification of watchlist/special mention category accounts

5. Monitoring of early warning signals

Appointing a relationship manager/credit officer. The relationship manager/credit officer is an official who is expected to have complete knowledge about the borrower, his business, his future plans, etc. This relationship manager has to keep in constant touch with the borrower and report all developments impacting the borrowable account. He is also expected to conduct scrutiny and activity inspections. In the credit monitoring process, the responsibility of monitoring a corporate account is vested with this officer.

'Know Your Client' profile (KYC). Most banks in India follow a system of preparing a 'Know Your Client' (KYC) profile/credit report. As a part of the 'KYC' system, visits are made to clients and their business units. The frequency of these visits depends on the nature and needs of the relationship.

Credit rating system. The credit rating system is essentially used to identify, measure and monitor the credit risk of an individual proposal. At the bank level, this credit rating system enables the tracking of the health of the complete credit portfolio of the bank. Most banks in India have put in place a system of internal credit rating. While most of the banks have developed their own models, a few banks have adopted credit rating models designed by rating agencies. Credit rating models take into account various types of risks associated with a prospective borrower. This exercise is generally done at the time of sanction of a new credit account and at the time of review/renewal of existing credit facilities.

Identification of watchlist/special mention category accounts. The grading of the bank's risk assets is an important internal control tool. The purpose of identification of potential NPAs is to ensure that appropriate preventive and corrective steps are initiated by the bank to protect against the loan asset becoming non-performing. Most banks have a system to put certain borrowable accounts under a watchlist or special mention category, if advances operating under adverse business or economic conditions are exhibiting certain distress signals. These accounts generally exhibit weaknesses that are correctable but warrant close attention from the bank. Putting such accounts into a watchlist or special mention category helps to give the early warning signals, which enable relationship managers or credit officers to anticipate credit deterioration and take the necessary preventive steps so that these do not turn into non-performing advances.

Monitoring of early warning signals. It is important to be sensitive to signals of credit deterioration. Banks monitor a host of early warning signals for identification of potential NPAs. Most banks in India have laid down a series of operational, financial and transactional indicators that could serve to identify emerging problems in credit payments at an early stage. Early warning signals can be classified into five broad categories:

1. Financial
2. Operational
3. Banking
4. Management
5. External factors

Finance-related warning signals generally emanate from the borrowers' balance sheet, income expenditure statement, statement of cash flows, statement of receivables etc.

Finance-related warning signals
1. Persistent irregularity in the account
2. Default in repayment obligation
3. Deterioration in liquidity/working capital position
4. Substantial increase in long-term debts in relation to equity
5. Declining sales
6. Operating losses/net losses
7. Rising sales and falling profits
8. Disproportionate increase in overheads relative to sales
9. Rising level of bad debt losses
10. Operational warning signals
11. Low activity level in plant
12. Disorderly diversification/frequent changes in plans
13. Non-payment of wages/power bills
14. Loss of critical customers
15. Frequent labour problems
16. Evidence of aged inventory/large level of inventory

Management-related warning signals
1. Lack of co-operation from key personnel
2. Change in management, ownership or key personnel
3. Desire to take undue risks
4. Family disputes
5. Poor financial controls
6. Fudging of financial statements
7. Diversion of funds

Banking-related warning signals
1. Declining bank balances/declining operations in the account
2. Opening of account with other banks
3. Return of outward bills/dishonoured cheques
4. Sales transactions not routed through the account
5. Frequent requests for loan
6. Frequent delays in submitting stock statements, financial data, etc.

Signals relating to external factors
1. Economic recession

2. Emergence of new competition

3. Emergence of new technology

4. Changes in government/regulatory policies

5. Natural calamities

Measures to reduce NPAs

Today, NPAs are a major drag on a bank's profitability. The reduction of NPAs to a significantly low level can strengthen the profitability of banks. A few suggestions that could help banks to do so are listed bow:

1. Recovery of loans should be linked with employees' performance appraisal; every bank as well as each branch must choose its own way to implement this.

2. Organisation of loan recovery camps with the help of local revenue authorities and *gram panchayats* can yield results.

3. A special recovery cell with committed staff and extra incentives on the basis of recovery performance should be set up.

4. Strengthening the Debt Recovery Tribunals (DRTs) with adequate staff and legal support can be considered. Borrowers that have small loans for recovery do not come under the DRTs at present. These tribunals should deal with all types of loans, and their geographical coverage should be extended.

5. Only those banks that are strongly committed to productivity and profitability should be transferred to the Asset Reconstruction Fund. Such banks may be allowed to write off a large volume of NPAs in a phased manner. The government should provide this benefit to such banks.

6. Banks should get some amount of operational freedom for lending. The stipulation of 'priority sector' lending can be relaxed on a case-to-case basis.

7. To improve the quality of lending, the design of lending schemes and the appraisal technique procedure for disbursement of loans should be based on applied research. Frequent exchange of information within and amongst banks in each region and across the regions should be encouraged.

An increase in the non-performing assets is not healthy for any bank. RBI has taken many steps to minimise the NPAs in India. For example, it has ordered banks to collect the interest on jewel loans once in three months. Banks must monitor their lending activities closely to minimise NPAs. They must use their funds optimally and follow innovative methods for debt collection.

The authors are assistant professors in the Department of Commerce (CA), Ayya Nadar Janaki Ammal College in Sivakasi, Tamil Nadu

BY: DR I. SATYA SUNDARAM

CEMENT: CAPACITY EXCEEDS CONSUMPTION

The removal of controls over the cement market has had both positive and negative results. Decontrolling has led to improved use of technology and higher efficiencies, yet allowed leading players to form cartels and control prices. The industry is also facing a deep crisis in terms of excess capacities.

Cement is an integral part of the core sector, and as such, crucial to the healthy growth of the economy. As the growth rate of the economy accelerates, demand for cement is bound to grow. In India, ever since the cement market was decontrolled in 1989, there has been a consistent spurt in demand as the government's hands-off stance facilitated the entry of new technologies into the industry. Quite a few players converted their plants from the wet to the dry process, which also improved efficiency. The industry could achieve 5 to 6 per cent growth from 2010-11 through to 2012-13.

However, the century old cement industry in India is now in deep crisis. The Working Group on the cement industry for the 12th Five Year Plan (2012-17) has concluded that the industry will have a capacity close to 470 million tonnes per annum by 2017.

Current status

Given the abundant availability of limestone, the country is capable of meeting the demand for cement for many years to come. The positive

developments over the recent past include the technological improvements and the huge pool of engineering talent. Also, demand is growing at 11 per cent on an all-India basis, and the per capita consumption is still low. Hence, the prospects for the cement industry are bright. In well developed countries, cement growth arises out of institutional buying, whereas in India, demand comes mainly from individual households.

India's cement industry performed well in the financial year 2011-12 thanks to the robust revival in demand during the second half of the year. The industry grew 6.4 per

cent in 2011-12 against a 5 per cent growth in 2010-11.

The industry sold 223.02 million tonnes of the building material in 2011-12 compared with 209.5 million tonnes in 2010-11. Production, too, rose to 223.5 million tonnes in 2011-12 against 210.5 million tonnes in 2010-11.

The cement industry in India had introduced various energy conservation initiatives throughout the manufacturing process. These include: improving the grinding techniques, modifications in the kiln firing system, upgradation of preheaters from the 4-stage variety to the 6/7-stage options, changes in the clinker grinding system, operating the manufacturing processes in a closed circuit system, and waste heat gases being liberated from kilns and coolers.

Experts say the cement firms' grip on pricing has weakened. In November 2012, the average all-India price was ₹ 295 for a 50 kg bag. After one year, in November 2013, it fell to ₹ 282, a decline of 4.5 per cent. There is obviously a mismatch in the pace of consumption of cement and capacity addition.

Some problems

The cement industry seems to have over-estimated demand and created excess capacities. The current overall capacity is around 360 million tonnes per annum. With a capacity addition of 10 per cent per year from current levels, the 12th Plan projection for capacity addition can be easily achieved. Amid lower cement off-take, capacity utilisation is below 75 per cent (in some regions, it is not more than 60 per cent). So is the industry heading towards a self-created mess?

One of the main problems faced by the cement industry is related to transport bottlenecks. The policy makers should pay special attention to this problem. Cement is a bulk product so its transport is cost intensive. Problems arise from the poor quality of roads, checkposts and outdated controls. The railway route has not proved helpful due to wagon shortage, material evacuation constraints and labour shortage.

The cement companies have to improve their internal rate of return (IRR) from the current rate of 9 per cent, if they need to attract funds for expansion. IRR is the rate at which an investment breaks even (with no profit and no loss).

Some studies have revealed that cement prices have not increased as much as production and capital costs over the last four years. The gap between operating costs and sales realisation has been coming down over the years.

The average EBITDA (earning before interest, tax, depreciation and amortisation) has declined from 17 per cent to 9 per cent for a green field cement plant, thanks to the steady rise in the cost of capital from ₹ 4200 a tonne in 2009 to ₹ 7200 in 2013.

The rise in the cost of production is attributed to a rise in power and fuel and gypsum costs, as well as in

Table I
Growth in Installed Capacities

(in million tonnes)

Year	Capacity
1950-51	3.26
1990-91	64.55
2000-01	132.90
2005-06	171.47
2006-07	179.06
2007-08	209.40
2008-09	225.00
2009-10	262.91
2013-14*	360.00

*Forecast

the cost of logistics and distribution. The wages for blue-collar workers have risen. It needs to be noted that the import of cement is now duty-free. The domestic players are thus at a disadvantage.

The cement companies have been accused of many malpractices. The Competition Commission of India (CCI) has observed that cement firms meet regularly to fix prices, control market share and hold back supply. The companies have been accused of entering into anti-competitive agreements in order to control the supply of cement. It is said the companies used the platform of the CMA (Cement Manufacturers Association) to indulge in collusive price fixing. The Director General (DG) of investigation came to the conclusion that the price of cement in the country is rising faster than that of its inputs. The price of cement has risen from ₹ 150 per bag in 2004-05 to ₹ 300 a bag by March 2011—even though during 2010-11, capacity utilisation has come down to 73 per cent.

In June 2012, the CCI imposed a penalty of ₹ 6300 million on 11 cement majors and the CMA. In May 2013, they were asked to pay a tenth of the penalty. The CCI found the firms guilty of forming cartels and manipulating prices in the market.

Table II
Cement Consumption Growth Patterns

(in million tonnes)

Year	Consumption	Growth (%)
2007-08	167.69	8.01
2008-09	180.95	7.91
2009-10	200.02	10.54
2010-11	209.61	4.79
2011-12	223.02	6.40
2012-13*	234.05	4.95

*Estimates

In the current context of widespread awareness about the environmental damage caused by certain industries, we have to pay attention to the ecological dimensions of cement manufacturing. The contribution of the cement industry to global warming is substantial. The industry has four major emissions—dust, sulphur dioxide, nitrogen oxide and carbon dioxide. Managing carbon dioxide emissions assumes importance in the coming years.

The way ahead

A major boost in demand should come from the housing sector, particularly in rural areas. However, an improved implementation of the National Rural Employment Guarantee Scheme and the Indira Awaas Yojana is needed. Projects relating to roads and highways, ports, railways and power, need to be completed on time. Also, cement companies should explore export options.

Special attention should be paid to issues arising from climate change. The focus should be on sector-specific and cross-cutting technologies, the use of bio-fuel, as well as the re-use of materials. Attention should also be paid to improving the energy efficiency of clinker manufacturing. ∎

The author is an economist and a regular contributor to Facts For You

BY: DR VIGNESHWARA VARMUDY

RADISH NEEDS ORGANISED MARKETING

Though radish is grown in abundance in India, and is relatively low priced, there is a need for planned cultivation, good storage facilities and a better marketing strategy for this nutritious vegetable.

The cultivation of radish (Raphanus sativus L.) originated in Europe and Asia, but today this vegetable is grown all over the world. Known for its pungent flavour, the tender tuberous roots of the radish are eaten raw as a salad or are cooked like a vegetable. The radish is believed to have originated from Raphanus raphanistrum, which is widely distributed as a weed crop in Europe.

Radish is very rich in minerals and vitamins. The roots and leaves of this vegetable are nutritious and found in abundance. Hence, this vegetable is relatively low priced in the market compared with other root vegetables, and consumed by both the upper and lower sections of society. It is very refreshing when eaten fresh, as it contains ascorbic acid and a variety of mineral salts. The seeds of the radish have non-drying fatty oil, which is suitable for soap making.

Health benefits

Like most vegetables, the radish, too, has quite a few health benefits and should be a part of your diet. Some benefits are:

1. It is a very good source of anti-

oxidants, electrolytes, minerals, vitamins and dietary fibre.

2. It contains an anti-oxidant compound called sulforaphane. Studies suggest that this compound helps to prevent prostate, breast, colon and ovarian cancers.

3. Fresh roots of radish are rich in vitamin C, which helps the body to scavenge harmful free radicals and boost immunity.

The nutrition value of radish in shown in Table I.

Radish cultivation in India

Radish is grown throughout India. West Bengal stands first in the area under cultivation and the production of radish, followed by Haryana, Assam, Bihar, Odisha, Punjab, Chhattisgarh and Karnataka. During 2012-13, the total area under this crop was 167.85 thousand hectares and the production was 2410.88 thousand metric tons. Table II gives the data on area and production of radish in the top 10 states in India.

The different varieties of radish

Radish varieties vary in shape, size and skin colour of the roots, and in the duration of the crop. The varieties can be divided into three groups—European or temperate, Asiatic or tropical, and Indian. The temperate varieties are small in size and excellent in quality. These are mainly used in salads. The tropical varieties are more pungent than their temperate counterparts and have large roots. An indigenous variety, the Jaunpuri Giant cultivated at Jaunpur in Uttar Pradesh, has roots that are 75-90 cm in length, 50-60 cm in girth and weigh up to 5-15 kg.

Some of the important improved Asiatic varieties cultivated today are *Pusa Deshi, Pusa Chetki, Pusa Rashmi, Japanese Whitel, Punjab Safed, Punjab Pasand, Punjab Agethi, Kalyanpur No.1, Arka Nishant* and *CO1*. The European varieties are *Pusa Himani, White Icicle, Scarlet Globe, Scarlet Long* and *Kashi Sweta*.

Harvesting and marketing

Depending upon the cultivar, radish roots are ready for harvesting 25-55 days after the sowing is completed. If harvesting is delayed, these roots turn bitter and pithy. After they are harvested, the roots are washed, tied into bundles and marketed along with the leaves. There is no organised marketing system for the radish in India, as there is in the case of many other vegetables.

Radish seed production

Seeds of European varieties are sown in the hills, and the tropical varieties are cultivated in the plains. Roots left *in situ*, without harvesting, produce the maximum quantity of seeds. For producing quality seeds, the roots are pulled out and true-to-type roots alone are re-

Table I
Nutrition Value of Radish
(per 100 grams)

Description	Value
Energy	16 Kcal
Carbohydrates	3.40 g
Protein	0.68 g
Total fat	0.10 g
Cholesterol	0 mg
Dietary fibre	1.6 g
Folates	25 ug
Niacin	0.254 mg
Pyridoxine	0.071 mg
Riboflavin	0.039 mg
Vitamin A	7 IU
Vitamin C	14.8 mg
Vitamin E	0 mg
Vitamin K	1.3 ug
Sodium	39 mg
Potassium	233 mg
Calcium	25 mg
Copper	0.050 mg
Iron	0.34 mg
Magnesium	10 mg
Manganese	0.069 mg
Zinc	0.28 mg
Carotene-B	4 ug
Carotene-O	0 ug
Lutein-Zeaxanthin	10 ug

Source: USDA, National Nutrient database

Table II
Area and Production of Radish in Top 10 States in 2012-13
(Third advance estimate)

States	Area (in '000 ha)	Production (in '000 metric tons)
West Bengal	40.60	496.20
Haryana	28.68	438.41
Assam	19.92	191.14
Bihar	16.42	271.82
Odisha	12.65	134.80
Punjab	11.73	240.07
Chhattisgarh	7.29	134.81
Karnataka	5.70	63.60
Uttarakhand	4.67	58.08
Jammu & Kashmir	3.63	81.45
Total (including others)	**167.85**	**2410.88**

Source: Ministry of Agriculture, Government of India

Table III
Top 10 Countries for the Export of Radish Seeds in 2012-13

Country	Quantity (in metric tons)	Value (in ₹ million)	Per cent share in total
Italy	85.26	9.03	41.39
Korea Republic	15.36	4.34	19.87
Vietnam Social Republic	13.04	1.31	5.99
Bangladesh	14.10	1.18	5.41
Cyprus	5.00	1.12	5.40
Pakistan	7.75	0.97	4.42
Oman	3.81	0.95	4.34
Egypt Arab Republic	13.00	0.67	3.06
Yemen Republic	3.21	0.65	2.97
Saudi Arabia	1.50	0.49	2.23
Total (including others)	**166.97**	**21.82**	**100.00**

Source: DGCIS Annual Export

planted. India exports as well as imports the seeds of radish.

Export of radish seeds

India exports radish seeds to Italy, Korea Republic, Vietnam, Bangladesh and other countries. The total exports during 2012-13 were 166.97 metric tons, valued at ₹ 21.82 million. Of the total exports, 41.39 per cent were to Italy and 19.87 per cent to Korea Republic, while the share of Vietnam, Bangladesh and Cyprus, each, was around 6 per cent. Table III gives data on the top 10 countries to which radish seeds were exported during 2012-13.

Import of radish seeds

India imports radish seeds from Korea Republic, New Zealand, France, Italy, Thailand, China Peoples' Republic and Vietnam Social Republic. During 2011-12, the total quantity of import was 139.79 metric tons, which came down to 86.46 metric tons in 2012-13. Data on the import of radish seeds during 2012-13 is given in Table IV.

Table IV		
Import of Radish Seeds into India in 2012-13		
Country	Volume (in metric tons)	Value (in ₹ million)
Korea Republic	55.30	24.98
New Zealand	15.59	2.95
France	3.70	2.34
Italy	11.61	2.28
Thailand	0.11	0.74
China Peoples' Republic	0.10	0.07
Vietnam Social Republic	0.05	0.02
Total	**86.46**	**33.38**

Source: DGCIS Annual Import

The challenges in radish cultivation

The four most important challenges to the greater cultivation of the radish in India are: pests and diseases, poor production technology, an under-developed marketing system and non-availability of storage facilities. As this vegetable has nutritional as well as medicinal values, there is an urgent need for a planned effort to improve the cultivation of radish in India. Farmers must also be educated in the pre- and post-harvest challenges of radish cultivation. ∎

The author is associate professor in economics at Vivekananda College in Puttur, Karnataka

BY: DR I. SATYA SUNDARAM

AQUACULTURE: HUGE UNTAPPED POTENTIAL

Aquaculture is employment intensive and fetches a good income for small farming systems. It can be the key to meeting the ever-increasing demand for fish and fish products. Fish, when grown in small ponds alongside paddy crops, can help farmers survive when crops fail. They can also help to turn the silt in the pond into organic manure.

Experts say aquaculture is going to be the mainstay of fish and fish-based production the world over. Most of the seas worldwide are over-exploited. Thus, development of aquaculture farming is a key to meeting the growing demand for fish and fish products. Also, the ratio of direct catch from the sea to aquaculture is gradually shifting in favour of the latter. Of course, India is placed in an advantageous position on both counts. The Indian Ocean is less exploited compared with other oceans. Fish production in the country is set to cross the 13-million tonne mark by 2016.

Growing importance

About 67 per cent of the total fish produced in India is consumed in fresh form due to low demand for value added fish products, and about 6 per cent is converted into fishmeal. Processed and dried fish account for 16 per cent of consumption, while a very small portion of less than one per cent is canned. At present, domestic demand for all types of fish, including fresh and processed, is stated to be about 7.5 million tonnes. The fisheries sector employs about 14.5 million people and earned for-

Fishermen with their catch

eign exchange to the tune of ₹ 129 billion in 2010-11.

Aquaculture has two main divisions: one, marine organisms and the other, fresh water organisms. Marine creatures such as shrimp and prawns are grown mainly for export, and fresh water fish such as carp, *katla* and *rogu* are grown for the local market.

Aquaculture in small farming systems provides high quality animal protein and essential fatty acids, vitamins and minerals at affordable prices, especially for vulnerable groups. It is also employment intensive.

Aquaculture production in the country reached an all-time high of 216,500 tonnes during 2011-12—an increase of 58 per cent over the previous year. Awareness created on the importance of maintaining quality and food safety in farmed shrimp by adopting good management practices in the supply chain has helped the sector to perform well, despite a number of hurdles.

Inland fish production contributes both to the domestic market and exports. While carps and other fish, caught either from rivers, lakes and reservoirs or cultured in ponds, largely provide for domestic consumption, shrimp and scampi, mainly from culture, bring the major share of the country's export earnings. This segment also provides for substantial livelihoods and employment generation in rural areas.

Amid leading coastal states in India, West Bengal is the top producer of fish with 1.61 million tonnes, followed by Andhra Pradesh with over 1.35 million tonnes annually.

Aquaculture in India has evolved as a viable farming practice over the last three decades, with considerable diversification in terms of species and systems. It has been showing

Table I
Inland Fisheries Resources in India

Rivers and canals (km)	195,210.00
Reservoirs (00,000 ha)	31.50
Tanks and ponds (00,000 ha)	24.14
Flood plains/derelict water bodies (00,000 ha)	8.20
Brackish water (00,000 ha)	12.40
Saline/alkaline affected areas (00,000 ha)	12.00

Table II
Inland Fish Production in India
(in million tonnes)

Year	Production
1990-91	1.50
2000-01	2.80
2003-04	3.40
2004-05	3.50
2005-06	3.80
2006-07	3.80
2007-08	4.20
2008-09	4.70
2011-12	5.22

an impressive annual growth rate of 6 to 7 per cent. The carp-based freshwater aquaculture—mainly constituted of Indian major carps like *katla*, *rohu* and *mrigal*—has been contributing over 90 per cent of the aquaculture production. The shrimp-based coastal aquaculture, with only about 5 per cent share, contributes to much of the export earnings.

Most fish in India are consumed fresh. The market for processed fish is limited in the domestic market, and is restricted to fish pickles, *papads*, cutlets and the like. A similar market exists for fish as an item of choice in high-end hotels in the country. Urbanisation, international trade reforms and rising per capita income have caused a diversification of food habits. Retail marketing is expected to have a positive significant effect on inland fisheries, particularly the segments of reservoir

The Global Scene

According to the biannual Food Outlook Report of the FAO, 2013, global fish prices rose to a record in 2013 due to rising demand for salmon and falling supplies of tuna. Prices for farmed fish such as salmon rose faster than those from capture fisheries. The FAO data show aquaculture production is predicted to climb 5.6 per cent in 2013, while capture of wild fish may rise 0.9 per cent.

According to FAO, salmon demand remains strong despite rising prices. There is a structural shift in consumer demand, which is positive for salmon producers. Despite record high prices, demand for tuna remains strong.

Total fish production is forecast to climb 2.9 per cent to 161.2 million tonnes in 2013 from 156.7 million tonnes in 2012, with aquaculture output climbing to 70.2 million tonnes from 66.5 million tonnes. The value of fish exports is predicted to climb 2 per cent to US$ 138 billion in 2012, after rising 0.5 per cent to US$ 128.2 billion in 2011. China, Norway and Thailand occupy the top three slots.

Global food consumption of fish is forecast to rise to 19.7 kg per capita in 2013 from 19.2 kg in 2012, mainly as consumers eat more farmed fish, according to the FAO report.

fisheries and freshwater aquaculture.

Compared to poultry farmers who require electricity 24 hours a day, fish farmers require electricity for only 5 to 6 hours once every 20 to 25 days to refill the pits with water. Also, compared to prawn and shrimp rearing, there is a very good demand for fresh water fish.

Along with fisheries, progressive farmers grow trees like coconut and banana. Digging ponds does not occupy a large area, as wrongly assumed by some. For instance, if 75 coconut trees are planted in one acre at a distance of about 7.62 metres (25 feet) between them, the same number of trees can be planted along the pond bunds at a reduced spacing of about 3.05-4.57 metres (10-15 feet) between them. The dried leaves of banana and coconut trees are mulched into the soil, and serve as good organic manure. This also prevents moisture evaporation. By continual mulching over the years, the salinity and the hard nature of the soil come down. Integrated fish farming cuts wastage and boosts income.

Aqua exports

India's aquaculture product ex-ports rose 54.2 per cent in volume, and 84.2 per cent in value terms in 2011-12, compared to those in 2010-11. Total exports were 244,500 tonnes, valued at ₹ 66,000 million, against 145,600 tonnes valued at ₹ 35,850 million in 2010-11.

The average price of aquaculture items was ₹ 300 a kg in 2011-12, up from ₹ 240 a kg in 2010-11. Around 27 per cent of the cumulative exports in 2011-12 were aquaculture products. This figure stood roughly at 10 per cent three years back.

Export demand is placed at 8 to 10 per cent of the total fish production in India. India's exports currently account for a meagre 2 per cent of the global trade in this sector.

Some challenges

Though there are several water conserving technologies available at present, farmers still largely depend on traditional methods for conserving water such as digging pits, and desilting ponds and tanks.

The marketing of inland fisheries in the country is facing problems of irregularity in the fish supplies, elasticities of the demand for the commodity, perishability of fish, and traditional practices adopted in marketing.

The other problems include: inadequate cold storage facilities, transport bottlenecks and high transport costs, presence of middlemen in the fish trade, lack of regulated market facilities, fluctuating fish prices, and seasonality of demand.

Marketing costs in upcountry markets account for the major share of the consumer rupee followed by profit margins for the middlemen. Also, the quality of the fish depends on the packing skills. The cost of packing depends on the type of containers, and the quality and type of ice used.

Current approach

Water management holds the key to the growth of aquaculture in India. The stress should be on minimal water wastage and increasing crop yield.

Progressive farmers say the government should encourage delta farmers to grow fish in ponds along with their paddy crops, as the income from the fish is three times more than that from paddy cultivation. Growing fish in ponds has a twin advantage: it provides a steady income for the farmers when their crops fail due to adverse conditions, and the silt at the bottom of the pit turns into a rich source of organic manure for the crops. Studies show the silt taken from a 30-cent fish pond can be used as a fertiliser for a one hectare field.

Contract farming, being taken up in other segments of agriculture, is expected to give the farmer a better deal, with proper guidelines. Entry of retail majors would also lead to the entry of related industries involved in fish and shrimp farming. The change in consumption pattern would provide a stimulus to the inland fisheries sector.

■

The author is an economist and a regular contributor to Facts For You

BY: DR ARPITA SHARMA

ALMOND: THE HEART-HEALTHY DRY FRUIT

Almonds eaten on a regular basis are a sure shot way of keeping good health. This dry fruit contains monounsaturated fats that will keep your heart young and active. The high magnesium and potassium content will help all the veins and arteries to relax and improve the flow of blood, oxygen and nutrients in the body.

The almond is the seed of the fruit of the almond tree, a medium-sized tree that bears fragrant pink and white flowers. Like its cousins, the peach, cherry and apricot trees, the almond tree bears fruits with stone-like seeds (or pits) within. The seed of the almond fruit is what we refer to as the almond nut.

The fruit of the almond is a drupe, consisting of an outer hull and a hard shell with the seed inside. Shelling almonds refers to removing the shell to reveal the seed. Almonds are sold shelled (i.e., after the shells are removed), or unshelled (i.e., with the shells still attached). Blanched almonds are shelled almonds that have been treated with hot water to soften the seed coat, which is then removed to reveal the white embryo.

Nutrients

Almonds are a very good source of vitamin E, manganese, biotin and copper. They are also a good source of magnesium, molydenum, ribofla-vin (vitamin B2) and phosphorus. Fortunately, although one-quarter cup of almonds contains about 11 grams of fat, a sizable portion of it (7 grams) is heart-healthy monoun-saturated fat.

Almond oil

Almond oil contains essential vi-tamins for skin health and beauty, including vitamin A, E and D. That is why many cosmetic products also use this oil as the primary ingredi-ent. To get the most beneficial effects of almond oil on the skin, it is neces-sary to mix it with other substances such as honey or other vegetable oils. Almond oil is used widely in many types of cosmetic products for the face, hair and skin. It contains plenty of the vitamins needed for our skin and hair to grow healthily.

Health benefits of the almond

Lowers LDL choles-terol and reduces risk of heart disease. Almonds are high in monounsaturated fats, the same type of health-promoting fats that are found in olive oil, which have been associated with reduced risk of heart disease. Almonds' ability to reduce heart disease risk may also be partly due to the antioxidant action of the vita-min E found in them, as well as to the LDL-lowering effect of almonds' monounsaturated fats.

When almonds are substituted for more traditional fats in human feeding trials, LDL cholesterol can be reduced by 8 to 12 per cent. In addition to healthy fats and vitamin E, a quarter-cup of almonds contains 62 mg of magnesium plus 162 mg of potassium. Magnesium is nature's calcium channel blocker. When there is enough magnesium around, veins and arteries breathe a sigh of relief and relax, which lessens resistance and improves the flow of blood, oxygen and nutrients throughout the body. Potassium, an important electrolyte involved in nerve transmission and the contraction of all muscles including the heart, is another mineral that is essential for maintaining normal blood pressure and heart function. Almonds promote your cardiovascular health by providing 162 mg of potassium and only 0.2 mg of sodium, making them an especially good choice in protecting against high blood pressure and atherosclerosis.

Almonds provide double-barreled protection against diabetes and cardiovascular disease. Reduction of after-meal surges in blood sugar helps to protect against diabetes and cardiovascular disease, most likely by lessening the increase in cholesterol damaging free radicals that accompanies large elevations in blood sugar. This is one reason why low-glycemic index diets result in lower risk of diabetes and heart disease. Almonds appear to not only decrease after-meal rises in blood sugar, but also provide antioxidants to mop up the smaller amounts of free radicals that still result. Eating almonds reduces the glycemic index (GI) of the meal.

Almonds' healthy fats may help to lose weight. An almond-enriched low calorie diet (which is high in monounsaturated fats) can help overweight individuals shed pounds more effectively than a low calorie diet high in complex carbo-

Almond tree with fruits

hydrates. Those on the almond-enriched low calorie diet consume 39 per cent of their calories in the form of fat, 25 per cent of which is monounsaturated fat. In contrast, those on the low calorie diet high in complex carbohydrates consume only 18 per cent of their calories as fat, of which 5 per cent is monounsaturated fat, while 53 per cent of their calories are derived from carbohydrates. Both diets supply the same number of calories and equivalent amounts of protein.

Eating almonds lowers risk of weight gain. Although nuts are known to provide a variety of cardioprotective benefits, many avoid them for fear of weight gain. A prospective study published in the journal *Obesity* shows such fears are groundless. In fact, people who ate nuts at least twice a week were much *less* likely to gain weight than those who almost never ate nuts.

Almonds help with energy production. Almonds are a very good source of manganese and copper, two trace minerals that are es-

sential co-factors of a key oxidative enzyme called *superoxide dismutase*. Superoxide dismutase disarms free radicals produced within the mitochondria (the energy production factories within our cells), thus keeping our energy flowing. Fortunately, Mother Nature supplies both mineral co-factors in almonds.

Riboflavin (vitamin B2) also plays at least two important roles in the body's energy production. When active in energy production pathways, riboflavin takes the form of flavin adenine dinucleotide (FAD) or flavin mononucleotide (FMN). In these forms, riboflavin attaches to protein enzymes called *flavoproteins* that allow oxygen-based energy production to occur. Flavoproteins are found throughout the body, particularly in locations where oxygen-based energy production is constantly needed, such as the heart and other muscles. Riboflavin's other role in energy production is protective. The oxygen-containing molecules the body uses to produce energy can be highly reactive and can inadvertently cause

damage to the mitochondria and even the cells themselves.

Almonds help to build strong bones and teeth. The phosphorus in almonds helps to make this possible.

Almonds help to provide good brain function and nourish the nervous system. Almonds contain riboflavin and L-carnitine, nutrients that boost brain activity and may also reduce the risk of Alzheimer's disease. They also nourish the nervous system. According to Ayurveda, almonds help to enhance intellectual levels and aid in longevity.

Benefits of almond oil

Useful as a scrub. Almond oil is an excellent carrier of salt and sugar, and is great for a facial scrub. In general, the salt or sugar works by removing dirt and rough or dead skin cells from the face. Almond oil works by immediately moisturising the scrubbed skin. A mix of almond oil with sugar is also effective to soften the lips.

Can be used for facial massage and to get rid of dark circles under the eyes. The best time to use almond oil for facial massage is before one goes to bed. This ensures that the oil will stay long enough so that it can perform its functions well. Almond oil massage helps to reduce dark circles under the eyes, removes dead skin cells and improves the texture of facial skin. For optimum results, we need to perform this treatment every day for several weeks. This treatment will not only get rid of dark circles under the eyes, but also help to reduce dark patches on the eyelids and crow's feet.

Cleanser. People with acne problems or sensitive skin should not use almond oil as a facial scrub, but they can use the oil as a facial cleanser. They can apply almond oil directly to the face and leave it for several minutes. Almond oil facial cleanser removes dirt as effectively as the facial scrub. Basically, the cleanser opens pores, which forces dead skin cells and dirt to come up to the surface.

Facial moisturiser. The most common benefit of almond oil for the face is that it can be used as a daily moisturiser. It not only softens rough or dry skin, but also creates a protective layer on the face. Wet your hands with warm water, and then massage the oil to all areas of your face. This will help the oil to penetrate more easily into the skin. Almond oil is a natural substance, so it is generally healthier since there is no chemical ingredient exposed to our facial skin.

The author teaches at G.B.P.U.A&T in Pantnagar, Uttarakhand

BY: M.J. SENTHIL KUMAR
DR P. SUNDARA PANDIAN

WHY DO EMPLOYEES LEAVE AN ORGANISATION?

This article takes a look at the reasons for employee turnover in an organisation, with special reference to the printing industry. It also highlights the role the management can play in retaining its best people.

When an organisation loses employees, it loses skills, experience and "corporate memory." The magnitude and nature of these losses is a critical management issue, affecting productivity, profitability, as well as product and service quality. A high level of employee turnover can negatively affect employee relationships and morale in the work place. The cost of replacing workers can be high, the problems associated with finding and training new employees can be considerable, and the specific skills and knowledge people walk away with can take years to replace. So organisations need to adopt strategies for retaining their employees, not only to increase productivity but also to maintain peace at the work place.

Statement of the problem

A certain level of labour/employee turnover allows for fresh ideas and energy in an organisation. But when the rate of turnover is high, its implications can be far-reaching and can lead to lapses in quality, increasing customer complaints, poor execution of orders, increased labour problems, etc. The company risks losing its reputation as well as market share. The management, therefore, has to monitor the reasons for high employee turnover and put in place corrective measures as soon as possible.

In Sivakasi in Tamil Nadu, companies in the printing industry experience employee turnover that is much higher than in other industries, and many entrepreneurs are under considerable stress on this account.

Scope of the study

Sivakasi is famous for the production of fireworks and safety matches, and for its printing presses. Nearly 90 per cent of India's fireworks and 80 per cent of India's safety matches are made in Sivakasi. And about 60 per cent of India's offset printing solutions are offered in Sivakasi. In short, Sivakasi is a big industrial centre in Tamil Nadu state, and pays high sales/excise/customs duties. On witnessing the industriousness of the people in this town, Pandit Jawaharlal Nehru, the first Prime Minister of India, had called Sivakasi a "mini Japan."

This town has a very active printing industry that is involved in the printing and publication of books, newspapers, wall posters, pictures

A printing press in Sivakasi, Tamil Nadu

and diaries. This industry provides abundant employment opportunities to the people living in Sivakasi, but leads in employee turnover.

Review of literature

Hom & Kincki (2001) discuss the causes of employee turnover in a paper titled 'Inter-role conflict and job avoidance'. Inter-role conflicts refer to multiple roles played by the employee and the stress accompanying these roles, which decreases the job satisfaction and increases the likelihood of the employee leaving the company.

Sheehan (1995) says that people leave their job for a better job. Employees are looking for a better opportunity, and do not suffer from job dissatisfaction. The needs of the employee, like health, family problems, financial needs, etc, are also reasons for leaving a job, and have an effect on the employee turnover.

Objectives of the study

The study in this article is undertaken to analyse the reasons for employee turnover in the printing industry in Sivakasi Taluk. The following are the main objectives of the study:

1. To evaluate the level of job satisfaction for an employee in the printing industry.

2. To evaluate employee behaviour when there is a certain level of job dissatisfaction.

3. To find out the reasons for employees leaving an organisation.

4. To analyse the current status of labour turnover in the printing units in Sivakasi.

5. To give suggestions on how to reduce the employee turnover rate.

Research design

Methodology. The present study is descriptive in nature. To fulfill the objectives of the study, both primary and secondary data have been used.

Primary data. The primary data was collected directly from the employees through well-structured interviews, conducted by the researchers.

Secondary data. The secondary data is an integral part of any research study as it provides information on key variables. The secondary data was collected from articles, journals, dailies and unpublished reports.

Statistical tools. Various statistical tools are used to analyse the primary data in a study. The researcher mainly used the percentage, rank correlation, point methods and Chi-Square test to analyse and interpret the data collected.

Sampling design. More than 50,000 workers are engaged in the printing and allied industries in Sivakasi. Due to the paucity of time, the researcher adopted a convenient sampling technique in which 175 employees were selected for the study.

Analysis and interpretation

Gender and educational classification. The work attitude and behaviour changes from one employee to another, based on the sex as well as the educational qualification. The information collected on the gender and educational qualification of the respondents is shown in Table I.

Table I shows that 72.57 per cent of the respondents are male, of

Table I
Gender and Educational Status of the Employee

Gender	Number of respondents				Total	Percentage
	Up to primary education	Up to higher secondary education	Diploma holders	Degree holders		
Male	26	53	27	21	127	72.57
Female	22	21	2	3	48	27.43
Total	48	74	29	24	175	100.00

Source: Primary Data

Table II
Work Experience

Experience	Number of respondents	Percentage
Less than 5 years	20	11.42
5 to 10 years	52	29.71
10 to 15 years	68	38.87
More than 15 years	35	20.00
Total	175	100.00

Source: Primary Data

which 41.73 per cent (53 out of 127) are educated up to the higher secondary level.

Work experience of the employee. The employees are classified into skilled, semi-skilled and unskilled categories based on their experience and work knowledge. Table II puts together information gathered with respect to the work experience of the 175 employees included in this study.

Table II shows that 11.42 per cent of the employees have less than five years' experience, 29.71 per cent possess 5 years' to 10 years' experience, 38.87 per cent have experience between 10 and 15 years, and the remaining 20 per cent of the employees have more than 15 years of work experience.

Reasons for joining a new company. An employee chooses to join a particular industry for specific reasons, which may differ from one

Table III
Reasons for Joining a Particular Company

Reasons	Number of respondents	Percentage
Attractive salary as compared to the previous company	52	29.71
Better working hours	21	12.00
More welfare benefits	25	14.28
More chances of career development	16	09.14
Attractive company rules and regulations	24	13.72
Availability of recreation facilities and freedom	37	21.15
Total	175	100.00

Source: Primary Data

Table IV
Loyalty to the Company

Loyalty	Number of respondents	Percentage
Will continue with current company	62	35.43
Will not continue with current company	113	64.57
Total	175	100.00

Source: Primary Data

Table V
Reasons for Leaving an Organisation

Reasons	I Rank	II Rank	III Rank	IV Rank	V Rank	VI Rank	VII Rank	Total
Low salary	33	30	23	15	8	4		113
Long working hours	27	21	18	13	10	13	11	113
Poor working conditions	13	20	19	23	19	13	6	113
Poor relationship with supervisor	7	8	18	25	20	16	19	113
Strict rules and regulations	10	4	6	13	27	31	22	113
Improper communications	4	9	8	11	22	27	32	113
Inadequate incentives	19	21	21	13	7	9	23	113
Total	113	113	113	113	113	113	113	

Source: Primary Data

person to another. The researcher gathered information on the reasons for people taking up a job in the printing industry in Sivakasi. The results are displayed in Table III.

Table III shows that the most important factor for people joining a particular company is a higher salary. Other factors, in the order of importance, are: availability of recreation facilities and relative freedom in the workplace, more welfare benefits, attractive rules and regulations, and better working hours. Only a small percentage of workers (9.14 per cent) gave importance to career development!!

Employees may continue in the same company or leave it based on their need fulfillment. So the study collected information on whether the respondents liked to work in the same organisation for a long period of time. This information is presented in Table IV.

Table IV shows that 35.43 per cent of the 175 employees would like to continue their services in the same company, while the remaining 64.57 per cent of the respondents would like to leave the institution in the near future.

Reasons for leaving. As shown earlier, of the 175 employees interviewed for this study, 113 employees were not willing to continue their services in the same institution. To ascertain the reasons for leaving, a study was made and the responses analysed by adopting the ranking method. The results are given in Table V.

It can be seen from this table that as many as 33 people ranked low salary and only 4 out of 113 people ranked improper communications as the number one reason for leaving an organisation. Table VI lists the weighted average points deduced from the results in Table V, in order to arrive at a ranking of the various reasons for employees leaving an organisation. This ranking has been worked out by assigning marks to each rank (10 marks for Rank I, 9 marks for Rank II, and so on), and dividing the total marks in each category (1 to 7) by the number of respondents.

From Table VI, it can be inferred that the main reason for employee turnover in an organisation is a low salary, followed by the working conditions and the relationship with the supervisor. 'Inadequate incentives' was the fourth most important reason for employees leaving an organisation, followed by long working hours, strict rules and regulations, and improper communications, in that order. It's interesting to note that while only 13 people out of 113 (Table V) ranked 'poor working conditions' as the number one reason for leaving an organisation, this was ranked as the second most important reason once the weighted average points were taken into consideration (Table VI).

Method of leaving. Next, the study collected information on whether employees in this sample gave prior notice before leaving the job. Table VII shows the results of the study.

From this table it is clear that of the 113 employees interviewed, only 15.04 per cent said they would give prior notice and leave the organisation, and the remaining 84.96 per cent said they would quit their job without any prior information.

The warning signs. Employees who plan to leave a job give out a few warning signs before they actually do so. If employers put some systems in place to recognise these signs, they would be better prepared for the eventuality and could also prevent rapid employee turnover. Information collected in this study, with respect to the warning signs employees give before they actually resign, is set out in Table VIII.

From Table VIII it can be seen that 14.16 per cent of the respondents expressed their job dissatisfaction by increasing wastages, 51.33 per cent of the employees availed frequent leaves without any information, 18.59 per cent reduced their productivity, 7.07 per cent created unwanted problems in the work place, and the remaining 8.85 per cent indulged in misbehaviour to communicate their dissatisfaction.

A few suggestions for employers

This study brings to light a few pointers that employers could keep in mind in order to reduce employee turnover in their organisations. These are:

1. As salary is the key reason for employee turnover, businesses must frame an attractive wage system.

2. To attract and retain its employees, a company must provide attractive incentives to its workers in addition to the salary.

3. Companies must adopt proper recruitment and selection processes to ensure employees are given jobs that match their skills.

4. Companies must conduct training programmes to enhance the skills of their employees. These training programmes should also focus on enabling good relationships in the organisation and enhancing communication skills. They should train employees to abide by company rules and regulations.

5. Organisations should try and provide transport facilities to their employees, especially if they have to commute from rural areas.

6. Good working conditions are extremely important. Factories and offices must have adequate ventilation facilities, exhaust fans, flood lights, etc, which take care of the employees' health.

7. A harmonious relationship between the management and the workers enhances productivity and reduces employee turnover.

8. An open door policy, which allows employees to talk about the challenges they face at work, will help to reduce stress at the work place.

To maintain healthy growth, the top management in every organisation must consider its employees as fixed assets. Frequent replacement of workers can be expensive for any business. There are direct as well as indirect costs of replacing workers and employees, apart from the loss of productivity in the transition period—the period between one employee's resignation and the complete training of the employee replacing him. Some employees that leave an organisation harm it further by taking away some of the old company's clients or customers. Organisations, therefore, need to have all the correct measures in place to avoid rapid employee turnover, and should also have the systems in place for proper employee replacement. All the efforts should be focused on maintaining and increasing job satisfaction to prevent rapid employee turnover.

■

M.J. Senthil Kumar is associate professor in the Department of Commerce (UG) at Sri Kaliswari College (Autonomous) in Sivakasi, Tamil Nadu. Dr P. Sundara Pandian is the principal of VHNSN College (Autonomous), Virudhunagar, Tamil Nadu

Table VI
Final Ranking of the Reasons for Leaving an Organisation
(based on weighted average points)

Reasons	Weighted average points	Rank
Low salary	8.469027	I
Poor working conditions	7.637168	II
Poor relationship with supervisor	7.309735	III
Long working hours	6.522124	V
Strict rules and regulations	6.017699	VI
Improper communications	5.814159	VII
Inadequate incentives	7.230088	IV

Source: Primary Data

Table VII
Procedure Adopted for Leaving the Job

Procedure	Number of respondents	Percentage
Prior notice	17	15.04
No prior information	96	84.96
Total	113	100.00

Source: Primary Data

Table VIII
Warning Signs of Impending Employee Resignation

Symptoms	Number of respondents	Percentage
Increased wastages	16	14.16
Frequent leaves without information	58	51.33
Reduced productivity	21	18.59
Creating problems in the work place	8	7.07
Misbehaviour and lobbying in the work place	10	8.85
Total	132	100.00

Source: Primary Data

BY: B. RAMACHANDRAN

FRAUDS IN THE BANKING SECTOR: AN OVERVIEW

Bank fraud is not a new phenomenon. But the extensive use of technology by banks today does give this fraud a new dimension and the power to cause extensive financial damage. Banks, therefore, have to be very proactive in setting up strong guidelines and policies to prevent and check these frauds. The RBI is helping them do just that.

Bank fraud is the use of potentially illegal means to obtain money, assets or other property owned or held by a financial institution. In many instances, bank fraud is a criminal offence. While the specific elements or particular banking fraud laws vary between jurisdictions, the term bank fraud applies to actions that employ a scheme or artifice, as opposed to bank robbery or theft. For this reason, bank fraud is sometimes considered a white-collar crime.

Defining fraud

Fraud has been defined as "... a deliberate act of omission or commission by any person, carried out in the course of a banking transaction or in the books of account maintained manually or under computer system in banks, resulting in wrongful gain to any person for a temporary period, or otherwise, with or without any monetary loss to the bank." (Report of the 'Study Group on Large Value Bank Frauds' issued by RBI.)

The word 'fraud' has also been defined in the Indian Contract Act. In short, fraud is dishonesty leading to loss to someone. Dishonesty is never accidental. Hence, there is always a swindler behind each bank fraud. The number of bank frauds in India is substantial and is increasing with the passage of time. Bank frauds are due to the bunko and the bungler bankers, situational pressures, and permissive attitudes. Fraud has not been defined in the Indian Penal Code directly. However, sections dealing with cheating, concealment, forgery, counterfeiting, misappropriation and breach of trust cover the same adequately.

Types of fraudulent acts

Fraud can be committed through many media, including mail, wire, phone and the Internet (computer crime and Internet fraud). The international reach of the Web and the ease with which users can hide their location, the difficulty of checking identity and legitimacy online, and the simplicity with which hackers can divert browsers to dishonest sites and steal credit card details have all contributed to the very rapid growth in Internet fraud. In some countries, tax fraud is also committed through false billing or tax forgery. There have also been fraudulent 'discoveries', for example, in science, to gain prestige rather than immediate monetary gain.

The BBC World service reported in 2012 that the estimated value lost through fraud in the UK was US$ 100 billion a year. The Fraud Act 200 is an Act of the parliament of the UK. It affects England, Wales and Northern Ireland. It was given Royal Assent on November 8, 2006, and came into effect on January 15, 2007.

The US government's 2006 fraud review concluded that fraud is a significantly under-reported crime, and while various agencies and organisations attempt to tackle the issue, greater co-operation was needed to achieve a real impact in the public sector. The scale of the problem pointed to the need for a small but high-powered body to bring together the numerous counter-fraud initiatives that existed.

Types of banking fraud

As a customer we may be seen as a potential target for fraud. However, by arming ourselves with information and a few tools, we can protect ourselves from becoming a victim of fraud. Let's take a look at

the various types of banking frauds and how we can protect ourselves from them.

Electronic fraud. Here are a few pointers to keep us protected from this kind of fraud.

1. Our bank accounts should be reconciled promptly and regularly.

2. We should never sign blank cheques.

3. We must ensure that our signature is not on documents that can be accessed by the general public.

4. We must keep all cheque books secure when not in use to deter theft.

5. When writing a cheque, we should not leave gaps in the completion of the payee name, amount in words and in figures. If cheques are lost or stolen, 'Stop payment' instructions should be effected immediately. We must ensure that all invoices are valid before we pay them. We must consider electronic means of payment (if possible) for high value payments.

6. We must ensure that our mailbox is secure to safeguard the cheques we receive.

Identity theft. Information with respect to our identity can be stolen in various ways. These include theft from our mailbox at home (utilities bills, etc), information given away by throwing used credit cards/debit

cards without destroying them in our garbage bins, and hackers on the Internet.

Credit/debit card related frauds. To avoid frauds arising from the misuse of our credit or debit cards, we must memorise our personal identification number (PIN) and carefully check all our card statements. Credit cards should not be left out of sight, and must be signed immediately on receipt from the bank.

Cheque fraud. Cheque fraud is the use of a cheque to get financial advantage by:

1. Stealing and altering a legitimate cheque (payee/amount) without authority.

2. Duplication or counterfeiting of cheques.

3. Using false invoices to get legitimate cheques.

4. Depositing a cheque into a third party account without authority.

5. Handing a cheque payment knowing that funds in the account are insufficient to cover the cheque.

In a report filed by Sandeep Pai and Mahua Venkatesh in the *Hindustan Times*, New Delhi, on January 30, 2014, it was stated that public sector banks have cumulatively lost a sum of ₹ 227.43 billion due to cheating and forgery in the last three years!! This information was received in response to a right to information (RTI) application.

The Reserve Bank of India has classified banking frauds on the basis of the provisions of the Indian Penal Code (IPC) as follows:

1. Misappropriation (Section 403 IPC) and criminal breach of trust (Section 405 IPC);

2. Fraudulent encashment through forged documents, manipu-

lation of books of account or through fictitious accounts and conversion of property (Section 477 A, 378 and 120A);

3. Unauthorised credit facilities extended for reward or for illegal gratification;

4. Negligence and cash shortages;

5. Cheating (Section 415 IPC) and forgery (Section 463 IPC);

6. Irregularities in foreign exchange transactions; and

7. Any other type of fraud not coming under the specific heads as above.

Technology has become an integral part of banking. Technology-driven frauds are becoming common in India also. Internet frauds in India are a recent phenomenon but are slowly turning into organised crime. Hackers can cross geographical boundaries and commit fraud. Banking transactions on the mobile are also being hit by these frauds.

There are three crucial elements that are considered responsible for the commission of frauds in India:

1. Failure of bank staff to follow instructions and guidelines.

2. Bank employees working in connivance with outsiders to commit these frauds.

3. Collusion between various external parties or by a hacker.

Proactive steps needed to monitor banking frauds in India

The evolving fraud landscape around banking and the increase in fraud-related losses requires automated detection systems and robust fraud defence processes. Buying an off-the-shelf system may not equip the bank with the most effective or strategic methods to deal with frauds. Selecting the right framework (and a seamless integration of bank systems with this framework) is integral to safeguarding business and customer interests.

According to data released by the RBI, banking related frauds doubled in the five-year period between 2004 and 2009. In 2009, the total number of bank frauds was recorded at 23,914, amounting to a loss of ₹ 18.83 billion.

With acquisitions and expansions spurring the growth in size and customer base of organisations, banks are witnessing a substantial rise in the numbers and complexity of fraud scenarios. Therefore, there is a stringent need for strong monitoring of all financial transactions routed through a bank.

RBI has directed financial institutions to continuously monitor transactions and set up an integrated fraud risk management framework. There is an increasing need to identify early warning signals to capture frauds close to their occurrence. A centralised framework can address fraud associated with various business units and products, and provide insights to stakeholders to take preventive action at the right time. This also eliminates uncertainty around losses due to fraud and helps the management have a more focused strategy to address fraud-related risks.

The impact on banks

There are instances of frauds that adversely impact banks on a regular basis and go unnoticed or un-attended. All these cases of fraud result in sizeable monetary losses for the banks if they go undetected.

Fraud events raise questions around the credibility of the fraud deterrent processes and the technological capabilities of the institution. External attacks on relatively newer channels such as Internet banking and mobile banking result in customer losses and hamper the brand image of the concerned entities.

RBI has been circulating to banks the details of frauds of an ingenious nature that have not been reported earlier, so that they introduce the necessary safeguards and preventive measures by way of appropriate procedures and internal checks. Banks are also being advised about the details of unscrupulous borrowers and related parties who have perpetrated frauds on other banks, so that they exercise caution while dealing with them. To facilitate this ongoing process, it is essential that banks report all frauds to RBI, giving the complete information and the follow-up action taken thereon. Banks should, therefore, adopt the reporting system for frauds as prescribed in the RBI Master Circular RBI-2013-14/88 dated July 01, 2013, and placed on the website of the RBI (www.rbi.org.in).

Banks must leverage the advantages of technology and accessibility of data to put in place a fraud mitigation system. A house is only as strong as its foundation and as weather-proof as its insulation. It is necessary, therefore, that a strong foundation is built by leveraging robust IT systems, framing effective policies and procedures, laying down strict compliance processes, setting high integrity standards, developing efficient monitoring, and initiating strict punitive action against the culprits in a time bound manner. It is also imperative that banks insulate themselves from unscrupulous activities by strengthening the fraud detection, mitigation and control mechanisms through prompt identification, investigation and exchange of information. This is necessary not just for the safety of banks, but for ensuring the stability and resilience of the overall financial system and sustaining the confidence that the various stakeholders have in its strength and integrity.

■

The author is assistant regional manager (retired), Central Bank of India, Madurai

BY: DR R. MANOHAR
M. MUTHUMARI
S. SHEIK ABDULLAH

THE IMPACT OF ADVERTISING ON THE INTERNET: A STUDY

The primary benefit of online advertising over traditional forms of advertising is that it reaches users across the globe. Also, an advertisement on the Net can be viewed 24×7. This article explores the potential of the Internet as a promotional tool for organisations, through a study done on a sample group Net users in the small town of Sivakasi in Tamil Nadu.

Online advertising promotes brands by using the Internet, mobile and other digital channels to reach consumers in a timely, personal and cost-effective manner. The success stories of a few companies that used Internet marketing have motivated many organisations to harness the potential of this new marketing channel. Advertising on the Internet is unique because it is interactive and can be customised to suit the viewing behaviour of the target audience.

In this article, the authors have made an attempt to analyse the effectiveness of Internet advertising through a study done in Sivakasi, Tamil Nadu on a sample of 140 Internet users. This study assesses the impact of Internet advertising on the purchasing behaviour of consumers.

Objectives of the study

The objectives of the study are:

1. To ascertain the importance of online advertising as a promotional tool

2. To ascertain which type of online advertising is preferred by consumers

3. To assess the effectiveness of online advertising on purchasing behaviour

4. To study the role of Internet advertising in creating awareness among consumers

5. To offer suitable suggestions to improve the effectiveness of online advertising

Sources of data

The primary data for the study has been collected through interviews with Internet users at various browsing centres in Sivakasi. The secondary data needed for the study has been collected from vari-

Table I
Gender-wise Classification of Respondents

Gender	Number of respondents	Percentage
Male	105	75.00
Female	35	25.00
Total	140	100.00

Source: Primary Data

Table II
Age-wise Classification of the Respondents

Age	Number of respondents	Percentage
Below 20 years	27	19.28
21-30 years	78	55.72
31-40 years	15	10.72
Above 40 years	20	14.28
Total	140	100.00

Source: Primary Data

Table III
Literacy Level of the Internet Users

Literacy level	Number of respondents	Percentage
Up to school	39	27.86
Diploma	31	22.14
Under-graduate	47	33.57
Post-graduate	23	16.43
Total	140	100.00

Source: Primary Data

Table IV
Nature of Employment

Employment status	Number of respondents	Percentage
Private employee	17	20.48
Self-employed	19	22.89
Professional	23	27.71
Business person	11	13.25
Government employee	13	15.67
Total	83	100.00

Source: Primary Data

Table V
Income of Respondents

Income (per month)	Number of respondents	Percentage
Less than ₹ 5000	15	10.71
₹ 5001-10,000	57	40.72
₹ 10,001-15,000	31	22.14
₹ 15,001-20,000	14	10.00
Above ₹ 20,000	23	16.43
Total	140	100.00

Source: Primary Data

Table VI
Knowledge of the Internet

Particulars	Number of respondents	Percentage
Yes	120	85.72
No	20	14.28
Total	140	100.00

Source: Primary Data

ous books, journals and magazines, related research reports and search engines.

The scope of the study is limited to Sivakasi alone. The judgment sampling method has been adopted for selecting the sample size of 140 Internet users in Sivakasi.

Analysis of the primary data

Gender-wise classification of

Internet users. Table I gives the gender-wise classification of the sample of 140 users. It is evident that 75 per cent are male users and the remaining 25 per cent are female users.

Age-wise classification of Net users. From Table II it is clear that most of the respondents (55.72 per cent) are in the age group of 21-30 years, followed by 19.28 per cent in the age group of below 20 years. Only 10.72 per cent of the respondents fall

in the age group of 31-40 years.

Literacy level of the Internet users. Table III shows that most of the respondents (33.57 per cent) are under-graduates while only 16.43 per cent are post-graduates.

Nature of employment. The occupation of the respondents is one of the factors influencing the effectiveness of Internet advertising.

It is evident from Table IV that most of the respondents are professionals, followed by the self-employed. Only 13.25 per cent of the respondents run their own businesses.

Income level of respondents. The browsing ability of Internet users varies with their income. The family income of the respondents is presented in Table V.

Of the 140 respondents, 40.72 per cent are earning ₹ 5001-10,000 and 22.14 per cent are earning ₹ 10,001-15,000 each month. Only 16.43 per cent of the respondents are earning above ₹ 20,000 per month.

Internet knowledge. Internet browsing requires a basic knowledge of computers and the various functions of the Internet. Table VI shows that most of the respondents (85.72 per cent) have adequate Internet knowledge.

Time spent on browsing. The time spent on browsing the Net differs from one person to another. It also depends on the speed of the Net as well as the respondent's ability to access it.

Table VII shows that most of the respondents (27.86 per cent) in the sample browse the Net for 2-3 hours, and almost the same number (27.14 per cent) use the Net for 1-2 hours in a day.

Amount spent on browsing. The amount spent on Internet browsing by the respondents is shown in Table VIII. It is evident from this table that most of the respondents spend between ₹ 41-60 per hour on browsing the Internet.

The purpose of browsing the Internet. The Internet is used to check emails, chat with friends, search information, shop online, and so on. Table IX shows what the 140 respondents in Sivakasi use the Internet for.

Not surprisingly, most of the respondents (32.86 per cent) access the Net for searching information. Only 19.28 per cent use the Net to chat.

The regularity of viewing Web advertisements. Table X shows that two-thirds of the respondents view Web advertisements with regularity.

What advertisements do the respondents look for? Table XI shows that most of the respondents are interested in viewing advertisements of consumer goods.

What kind of Web advertisements attract users? It is interesting to note that 50.72 per cent of respondents (Table XII) are fascinated by advertisements that use animation to communicate their message, and 25 per cent are attracted by interactive online advertisements.

Viewing habits. Internet users vary with respect to their viewing habits when it comes to Internet advertising.

Table XIII shows that 40 per cent of the respondents see a Web ad every day, and only 10.71 per cent see a Web advertisement rarely, if time permits.

How are purchase decisions made? Table XIV shows that of the 140 respondents interviewed for this study, 39.28 per cent made a purchase without consulting others, but as many as 36.43 per cent were influenced by advertisements on the Internet!

How many users make a purchase after seeing an advertisement on the Internet? Of the 140 respondents in the study, 52.14 per cent said that they made no purchase even after seeing advertise-

ments on the Internet. However, the remaining 47.86 per cent did make a purchase after seeing an advertisement on the Internet.

Types of goods preferred by the respondents. Table XV shows that most of the respondents (27.17 per cent) purchased textile materials, while only 12.86 per cent used information provided in the advertisements on the Internet to pur-

chase medicines.

The role played by advertisements on the Internet. Most respondents (28.57 per cent) felt that Internet advertisements played a role in reinforcing the familiarity of the product, 27.14 per cent felt that these advertisements play a role in convincing buyers to purchase a product, while 21.43 per cent felt that online advertising helps to

Table VII
Time Spent on Browsing

Duration	Number of respondents	Percentage
Less than 1 hour	34	24.28
1-2 hours	38	27.14
2-3 hours	39	27.86
More than 3 hours	29	20.72
Total	140	100.00

Source: Primary Data

Table VIII
Amount Spent on Browsing

Amount spent per hour	Number of respondents	Percentage
₹ 20	34	24.28
₹ 21-40	28	20.00
₹ 41-60	46	32.86
More than ₹ 60	32	22.86
Total	140	100.00

Source: Primary Data

Table IX
Purpose of Using the Internet Facility

Purpose	Number of respondents	Percentage
Search for information	46	32.86
Online shopping	34	24.28
Chatting	27	19.28
E-mail	33	23.58
Total	140	100.00

Source: Primary Data

Table X
Regularity of Viewing Web Advertisements

Particulars	Number of respondents	Percentage
Yes	93	66.43
No	47	33.57
Total	140	100.00

Source: Primary Data

Table XI
Advertisements that Users Look For

Advertisement preference	Number of respondents	Percentage
Consumer goods	33	35.48
Industrial goods	17	18.28
Commercial ads	21	22.58
Service ads	22	23.66
Total	93	100.00

Source: Primary Data

Table XII
Attractive Web Advertisements

Type of Web ads	Number of respondents	Percentage
Within the banner	27	19.28
Animation	71	50.72
Interactive advertisement	35	25.00
Non-Web advertisement	7	5.00
Total	140	100.00

Source: Primary Data

Table XIII
Viewing Habits of Net Users

Period	Number of respondents	Percentage
Every day	56	40.00
Once in three days	35	25.00
Rarely	15	10.71
Once in four days	34	24.29
Total	140	100.00

Source: Primary Data

Table XIV
Factors that Influence Purchase Decisions

Influences on purchase decision	Number of respondents	Percentage
Self	55	39.28
Family members	14	10.00
Friends	8	5.72
Relatives	12	8.57
Internet advertisements	51	36.43
Total	140	100.00

Source: Primary Data

Table XV
Types of Goods Preferred by the Respondents

Types of goods	Number of respondents	Percentage
Consumer goods	29	20.71
Industrial goods	25	17.86
Commercial goods	30	21.43
Medicines	18	12.86
Textile materials	38	27.14
Total	140	100.00

Source: Primary Data

introduce new products to the respondents.

Analytical framework

To analyse and put together the opinions of the respondents that have been tabulated above,

Table XVI
Internet Advertisements: Level of Satisfaction

Particulars	SA	A	NO	DA	SDA	Total	Cronbach Alpha
Get information about various products and services	35	69	7	21	8	140	0.898
Advertisements are attractive and creative	47	57	18	8	10	140	
See advertisements of reputed companies and websites while browsing	51	83	1	3	2	140	
Advertisements on Internet distract the attention of the Internet users	55	23	17	21	24	140	
Advertisements on Internet provide correct information and can be trusted	19	63	29	12	17	140	
Total	207	295	72	65	61	700	
Percentage	29.57	42.14	10.28	9.29	8.72	100	

Source: Primary Data
SA = Strongly Agree; A = Agree; NO = Neither Agree or Disagree; DA = Disagree; SDA = Strongly Disagree

Table XVII
Effectiveness of Online Advertisements

Statement	SDA	DA	NO	A	SA	Total	Cronbach's Alpha
Online advertisements attract me	11	55	15	28	31	140	0.851
Online advertisements arouse interest in the product/service	33	27	18	45	17	140	
Online advertisements tune the mindset to purchase a particular product	23	15	14	60	28	140	
Online advertisements lead to necessary action to purchase the product	37	56	9	15	23	140	
I am satisfied with the online purchase of a product/service	7	13	35	57	28	140	
Total	111	166	91	205	127	700	
Percentage	15.86	23.71	13.00	29.29	18.14	100	

Source: Primary Data
SA = Strongly Agree; A = Agree; NO = Neither Agree or Disagree; DA = Disagree; SDA = Strongly Disagree

with respect to the effectiveness of online advertising, the Likert five point scaling technique has been applied (with scaling options that range from 'strongly agree' to 'strongly disagree' allotted a score that ranges from 5 to 1; see Table XVI and Table XVII). After this, Cronbach's alpha test has been applied to evaluate the reliability of these statements. If the value of the Cronbach alpha is more than 0.7,

the statements/results are deemed reliable. The study found the alpha values for two statements—'level of satisfaction of Internet advertising' and 'effectiveness of online advertisements' to be 0.898 and 0.851, respectively.

Internet advertisements: level of satisfaction. Table XVI shows that 42.14 per cent of the respondents 'agree' while 29.57 per cent 'strongly agree' that advertisements

Salient Features and Findings of the Study

➤ Most of the respondents (75 per cent) are male.
➤ Most of the respondents (55.72 per cent) are aged between 21 and 30 years.
➤ Most of the respondents (27.86 per cent) spend 2-3 hours on browsing the Net every day.
➤ Of the 140 respondents, 46 respondents (32.86 per cent) spend ₹ 41-60 per hour on browsing.
➤ About 36 per cent of the respondents look for consumer goods while browsing.
➤ More than half of the respondents are attracted by animated advertisements.
➤ About 40 per cent of the respondents see Internet advertisements daily.
➤ Almost 40 per cent of the respondents take purchase decisions themselves without consulting others.
➤ About 27 per cent of the respondents purchase textile items after seeing the advertisement on the Internet.
➤ Most of the respondents (27.14 per cent) say that Internet advertisements make it convenient for them to purchase products online.

on the Internet provide a high degree of satisfaction to Net users with respect to the various parameters listed in the table.

Effectiveness of online advertisements. Consumers are increasingly relying on the Internet as a source of information on which they base their purchase decisions. Online advertising is proving to be an effective means for creating a brand and influencing consumers to make a purchase. The five point scaling technique was again used to measure consumer perception towards online advertising and its effectiveness.

Table XVII shows that nearly 30 per cent respondents 'agree' while 18.14 per cent 'strongly agree' that online advertising is effective with respect to the various parameters listed in the table.

A few suggestions

1. During the course of the study, it was found that a few respondents had no knowledge of the Internet. Periodic seminars, exhibitions and awareness programmes would help to improve people's knowledge about the Internet.

2. As most respondents are influenced by advertisements that have some animation in them, advertising agencies should look at creating such online advertisements.

3. Online advertising should be interactive and provide adequate details with respect to the product and company.

4. Advertisements should never mislead consumers about the product or service.

To sum up, the current audience that views advertising on the Internet is relatively small due to the present low level of awareness, but the strength of this audience should not be underestimated. With the Internet penetrating new areas every day, online advertising is the future. From the findings of the study in this article, it can be concluded that Internet users in even a small place like Sivakasi have a positive attitude towards online advertising. However, their satisfaction would depend on the effectiveness of the online advertisement and the need for the product or service.

■

Dr Manohar is associate professor, Post Graduate and Research Department of Commerce, A.N.J.A. College, Sivakasi. M. Muthumari is assistant professor of Commerce (Corporate Secretaryship) and S. Sheik Abdullah is a research scholar, Post Graduate and Research Department of Commerce in the same college

Cherries are not only delicious, but are also good for you. They have a lot of nutritional value, given the amount of calories they contain. There have been numerous research studies done on this fruit and the nutrients it contains, which indicate possible health benefits for those who consume cherries regularly.

BY: C. SIVAKKOLUNDU
DR P. LOGANATHAN

CONSUME CHERRIES FOR GOOD HEALTH

This tiny, red fruit is a powerhouse of nutrients. The high levels of potassium, magnesium and vitamin C that it has help to boost immunity and ease arthritic pains.

Types of cherry fruit

There are a number of types of cherries available. These include the sweet cherries that people often

Nutritional Facts

(Serving size 138 g)

Amount per serving	
Calories	87
Calories from fat	2

	Per cent daily value*
Total fat 0 g	0%
Saturated fat 0 g	0%
Trans fat 0 g	
Cholesterol 0 mg	0%
Sodium 0 mg	0%
Total carbohydrates 22 g	7%
Dietary fibre 3 g	12%
Sugars 18 g	
Protein 1 g	
Vitamin A	2%
Vitamin C	16%
Calcium	2%
Iron	3%

Per cent daily values are based on a 2000 calorie diet. Your daily values may be higher or lower depending on your calorie needs.

	Calories	2000	2500
Total fat	Less than	65 g	80 g
Sat fat	Less than	20 g	25 g
Cholesterol	Less than	300 mg	300 mg
Sodium	Less than	2400 mg	2400 mg
Total carbohydrate		300 mg	375 mg
Dietary fibre		25 g	30 g

Source: www.stemilt.com

buy in the grocery stores for eating fresh, as well as the sour variety that is often dried and used to make juices. Another type is the canned and sweetened maraschino cherries that are added on top of ice cream sundaes.

Two types of cherries are produced in the United States—sweet cherries and tart or 'sour' cherries. Washington, California, Oregon and Michigan are the primary sweet cherry producing areas, account-ing for more than 97 per cent of the quantity produced nationwide. The primary tart cherry producing state is Michigan, which alone accounts for nearly 90 per cent of the production of this type of cherry.

Consumption of sweet cherries

Cherries are consumed in a variety of ways, including fresh, frozen and canned, or as juice, wine, brined or dried. In recent years, two-thirds of the sweet cherries produced have been sent to the market for sale, with the remaining one-third used for processing. Of the sweet cherries that are processed, just over 50 per cent are brined.

Processing of tart cherries

Eighty-three per cent of the tart cherries produced in the US are used for processing, with the majority processed as a frozen product (67 per cent). A total of 16 per cent of tart cherries are canned, and the remainder (those that are neither frozen nor canned) are used for juice, wine, brined and dried products.

The marketing season for sweet cherries produced in the US lasts from early May to mid-August, while the marketing season for tart cherries lasts from mid-June to mid-August.

Nutrition data

Sweet cherries with pits have 113.5 calories per cup, as well as 2.9 g of fibre, 306 mg of potassium, 15 mg of magnesium, 0.5 mg of iron, 52 mcg of beta carotene and 9.7 mg of vitamin C, according to the USDA (United States Department of Agriculture) National Nutrient Database for Standard Reference. Sour cherries with pits have 88.7 calories per cup, as well as 16 g of fibre, 178 mg of potassium, 9 mg of magnesium, 33 mg of iron, 793 mcg of beta carotene and 0.3 mg of vitamin C.

Benefits

The high levels of vitamin C, potassium and fibre in cherries can help you to meet the recommended daily values for these nutrients. Vitamin C is essential for the immune system, as well as for providing antioxidant benefits. Potassium helps to balance electrolytes in the body and is important for proper functioning of the heart, kidneys, muscles and nerves. Fibre helps you feel full on fewer calories and also aids in the digestive process.

Studies have linked cherries to beneficial effects for those suffering from gout and arthritis, as well as possible preventive effects when it comes to certain cancers, diabetes and heart disease, according to the 'Choose Cherries' website. The site recommends one or two servings a day of fresh, dried or frozen cherries or cherry juice to get some of the possible disease-fighting benefits of these fruits.

Avoid the preservatives

When choosing cherries for health benefits, avoid the maraschino cherries. These cherries are full of added sugar, colour, flavour and preservatives. They are highly processed and are not a healthy option. Dried cherries remain nutritious, but since they are much more energy-dense than fresh cherries, they should be eaten in smaller amounts to limit the number of calories you are ingesting.

C. Sivakkolundu is assistant professor in the Department of Economics, Thiruvalluvar University, Vellore, Tamil Nadu. Dr P. Loganathan is associate professor and head of the Department of Economics, Kandasamy Kandars College, Namakkal, Tamil Nadu

The COMMUNITY SPIRIT

The community is the heart of civilised society. In recent years, it has suffered from a lack of care. In their concern for the quality of life, people lately have been rediscovering its value—and finding that their personal well-being and the community's are one and the same...

Nothing matters more to the mass of human beings than their need for one another. Our species would not exist, after all, if men and women did not mate. Beyond that, man is one of the few creatures to feel the need to mate for life and to gather his progeny around him in permanent families. Beyond that again, families have always answered a natural call to come together in groups.

This social instinct is the bonding agent of what we now call the community. The community has its roots in the family, which it resembles in many ways. It consists of individuals with common interests, common problems and roughly common values. But it is not just a big family. It depends much more on voluntary cooperation, and its members are free to choose whether or not to participate in it. The ties that bind it are looser and more fragile. It is more likely to go to pieces in the absence of conscious dedication, effort and care. The basis of a community may be territorial, religious, ethnic professional or what-have-you. The guiding philosophy in every case is that people are stronger together than they are apart. This should not be taken to mean that a community is merely a necessary evil. The origins of the word reflect

The community consists of individuals with common interests, common problems and roughly common values

its spirit: It comes from the Latin communis, which is composed of com, meaning 'together,' and munis, meaning 'ready to be of service' ... "Ready to be of service together"—that implies not only being in the same boat, but pulling in unison on the oars.

Certainly in the modern democratic sense of the term, a community is purposeful and dynamic. It draws its strength from a willingness on the part of its members to work together towards commonly agreed goals. At the back of this is a basic feeling of community which transcends all the practical benefits to be derived from cooperation. Like all feelings, it is difficult to describe precisely, but some of its ingredients are comradeship, tolerance, thoughtfulness and generosity. Whatever it is, this feeling is the driving force behind the kind of progressive community we know in this country today.

The most common form of community is that of a neighbourhood. Neighbourliness is fundamental to community life. But there is a difference between being a good neighbour and being a good member of the community. In a neighbourly relationship, you help the fellow next door on the understanding that he will help you if necessary. In your relationship with the community, you indirectly help everyone in it, and you do not expect to be repaid.

The chances are that anything you do for your community eventually will reap its reward in one way or another. At the very least, it is an investment in having an agreeable place to live. But the fact is that no community could function without people who consistently give more than they get—those invaluable toilers in the vineyard who organise events, who take the initiative and the responsibility, and who urge on the rest to greater things.

This readiness to serve and share is the badge of a civilised person. The opposite is selfishness, which is a distinctly uncivilised trait. In the primitive state of infancy, one of the first words a child will learn to say is 'mine'; violent disputes over toys and trinkets are waged before babies are out of diapers. Most parents (not all, unfortunately) train their offspring out of their selfishness as they train them out of their other anti-social habits. No community is without the flawed products of this system—self-seekers who want everything their own way.

For the most part, though, there is enough civility in the air to keep communities going. That the modern community exists at all represents a victory over the savage side of humanity. The earliest groups of human beings must have been much like packs of animals which were ruled by the strongest or most cunning members. The heirs to this tradition tried to take the curse off their crude extortion by claiming that, as superior be-

ings, they were entitled to the lion's share of other people's production by God-given right.

Lighting the beacons of democratic life

The pretence found its fullest expression in the feudal system of the Middle Ages. It was the very antithesis of the concept of the community. In a community, the rich help to support the poor and the strong the weak; that order was reversed under feudalism. The common folk were held in bondage to their lord and master. Historians tell us that the modern democratic community was conceived when traders and merchants of medieval Europe rebelled against this oppressive state of affairs.

Merchants in the market towns known as 'burgs' convened to write municipal charters setting out uniform rules governing trade and commerce. By doing so, they effectively stripped the feudal lords of their power. Once commercial order was established, civil order was not far behind; comprehensive penal codes were written. The *burgs* became oases of freedom and justice. In some, a serf could win his emancipation from bondage by staying a year and a day.

It was only the barest start, of course. As Lord Acton wrote in his *History of Freedom in Antiquity*, "In every age (liberty's) progress has been beset by its natural enemies, by ignorance and superstition, by lust of conquest and by love of ease, by the strong man's craving for power, and the poor man's craving for food." Injustice and inequity continued to abound; the march of civilisation was set back by wars, civil conflict, plagues and famines. Nevertheless, the seeds of some of the essential principles of modern community life had been sown.

A regressive community spins inward on itself

The overriding principle was that laws should be made with the agreement of those directly affected by them, and not by some detached autocrat acting by fiat. Implicit in this was the doctrine that there can be no proper authority without responsibility. If laws were to be made by people on the spot, they must be applied, administered and adjusted by those same people—or, in actual practice, by representatives answerable to them. Moreover, the laws must take account of local reality to the extent that the people subjected to them were willing to abide by them of their own free will.

The *burgs* and their satellite villages produced several other elements of the modern community. The division of labour, in which specialists took over tasks formerly performed in the home, made people realise how dependent on one another they were. It also helped

People are stronger together than they are apart

to promote equality. Writing of this period, sociologist Amos H. Hawley explained: "If functional interdependencies are to be relied upon, all parties must be treated as equals, at least under the law."

Division of labour gave rise to another prerequisite of community life—standardisation. The practical standards designed to facilitate trade were underpinned by ethical standards of fair dealing. A common understanding of what may and may not be done is imperative if people are to live harmoniously together. Where there is no code of conduct and no institution to enforce it, there is no peace.

Standards were set and policed by merchants and craftsmen's guilds, the forerunners of our present service clubs and chambers of commerce. In a way, these were communities in themselves—associations formed on the common ground of a particular trade. Their members were naturally concerned with establishing and maintaining orderly, prosperous conditions in their markets. Thus they began the first municipal works by undertaking such organised programmes as cleaning the streets where they kept their shops.

Guilds make an interesting study in the growth of institutions which are the vital organs of any community. But perhaps the most interesting thing about them is where they went wrong. At their zenith, they were genuinely community-minded; while they acted primarily in the interests of their members, they did much to improve conditions for the general citizenry. Then they became obsessed with perpetuating their monopolies and privileges. When they lost their public spirit, they slipped into decline.

The limits of utopia are set by human nature

The object lesson of the guilds lies in the fact that they stopped caring about the community. They came to act as factions, each fighting for its particular interest at the expense of everyone else. They went from being progressive to being regressive. A progressive community may be thought of as a spiral, spinning out concentrically in ever-widening circles. A regressive community has the same shape, except that it spins inward on itself.

In a regressive community, the natural tendency to think in terms of 'them and us' may be twisted into a mistrust—even a hatred—of others. The healthy feeling of pride in one's own kind may be channelled towards destructive ends. In contrast, progressive communities find constructive outlets for their pride by trying to be more friendly or efficient or neater than the next place. In sports and other competitive activities, they challenge each other to prove which is the better at a given place and time.

It is no accident that communities express themselves in acts of coordination such as a hockey team or a school band playing together. The ideal of teamwork is for everyone to perform his specialised part in conjunction with others towards a common cause; that is also the ideal of democratic community life.

The ideal community, however, has proved to be as much of a 'will o' the wisp' as the ideal hockey team in which the players never miss a pass or a scoring opportunity. The 19th century utopian communities in the United States and France failed ingloriously. If nothing else, these experiments proved that the limits of utopia are defined by what human nature will allow.

An intrinsic part of that nature is what William James has called 'the instinct of ownership.' In utopian communities, everybody's produce and property were pooled. Soviet communists subsequently extended this to the extreme of confiscating property and redistributing it throughout the population. By taking away the right of people to dispose of their own efforts and possessions as they saw fit, communism also took away the right to follow one's conscience and to assert one's individuality.

The communist experience has demonstrated that the community spirit cannot be forced; it thrives only when free men and women think for themselves in arriving at a consensus as to what is best for the majority. The difference between a commune and a democratic community is that members of the latter willingly participate in it; a community in which people had to be coerced into giving blood or holding a bake sale would not be a pleasant place to live in.

Neither would a place in which all the good works were performed by professionals. Until recently, it looked as if this might happen in Canada as part of centralisation of social, educational and municipal services and the formation of regional and metropolitan authorities. Economics dictated that small-scale localised institutions be replaced by larger units operated by central bureaucracies. Lately, however, the economics have changed: Necessary cutbacks in government spending have again assured us that there will be plenty of vital jobs for volunteers.

The urban revolt and a fresh look at values

Centralisation is only one of the trends in recent years that have threatened the survival of the progressive community. Quick, efficient transportation has created 'bedroom communities' whose commuter-inhabitants are detached from local concerns and activities. Television has tended to cut off contact among neighbours; the sort of people who once stood chatting on street corners may now be found glued to their sets in their living rooms. Commercial development has eradicated some urban neighbourhoods and left others as dilapidated areas with transient, rootless populations.

In fact, the strong roots which once nurtured the sense of community have been eroded everywhere in Canada as well as in other western nations. In a highly-mobile society, families have been scattered all over the map. The cultural homogeneity which held communities together has been diluted. The community spirit can no longer rest easily on the safe ground of sameness. Cultural diversity has called upon people to rise above the simple ethos of the tribe.

The pressures on the community are a direct cause of the psychological condition the experts call 'alienation.' Its sufferers feel left out of the system of mutual commitment and support. This feeling swelled to mass proportions in the United States in the 1960s when urban dwellers went on the rampage to burn and loot their own neighbourhoods. It has been said that the urban revolt was really a revolt against the indifference and impersonality of 20th century western society. The authorities sought a solution in strengthening neighbourhood institutions. In other words, they tried to redirect a community that had turned destructive back on to a constructive road.

The episode helped to bring about a reassessment of social values. This also took place in Canada, where many of the values are more or less the same as in the United States. Since then, the community spirit in both

It is no accident that communities express themselves in acts of coordination such as a hockey team or a school band playing together

countries has slowly been reviving. The movement seems to be in touch with the new reality. It recognises that, because of the many strong challenges to the community, ordinary citizens will have to try harder than ever to make their communities work.

Quality of life begins at home

Communities have learned to check the heavy hand of centralism by asserting themselves sharply when their interests are in danger of being overlooked in a bureaucratic shuffle. Imaginative new forms of participation and service—'walkathons' and the like—have been devised. Cultural diversity has been turned to advantage to broaden the outlook and deepen the character of communities. Rundown neighbourhoods are being repopulated and attractively restored.

The revival has drawn impetus from the current quest for a better quality of life. People are beginning to realise that the quality of life begins at home. It obviously depends to a large degree on how much they are willing to cooperate and share in the pursuit of common objectives. If they cannot cooperate and share more in their immediate neighbourhoods, how can they expect to improve the quality of life throughout the world?

It all comes down to the community spirit. That spirit is made up of helpfulness, consideration, accommodation and mutual respect. If it could ever come to rule the conduct of human affairs, men and women might yet live to see peace on earth as a permanent condition.

Courtesy: The Royal Bank of Canada

FUNDAMENTALS OF BUSINEES ORGANISATION & MANAGEMENT

Authored by Prof. Y.K. Bhushan; published by Sultan Chand & Sons, 23 Daryaganj, New Delhi 110002; soft cover; price ₹ 400.

This nineteenth revised and enlarged edition of the book was first published in 1963. The author did his M.Com from Delhi University and MBA from Indiana University in the USA. A Fulbright scholar, he has spent over 55 years in commerce and management education.

The book has been divided into nine parts to cover business system, ownership of business, company management, management principles, production, human resource, marketing, finance and environment. Each part deals with the subject in an exhaustive manner under several chapters.

For instance, in part five, which covers production function of management, the book explains in detail plant location, produc-tion planning and control, work improvement and work measure-ment, materials management, and the economics of size.

In part seven, which covers marketing function of management, the book systematically explains such subjects as marketing functions, pricing policies, channels of distri-bution, sales and advertising, insur-ance and transport, organised com-modity markets, and international marketing.

Though it seems to have been written primarily for students, the book could also serve as a valuable source of reference for mid-level cor-porate managers.

STRATEGIC MANAGEMENT

Authored by P.K. Ghosh; pub-lished by Sultan Chand & Sons, 23 Daryaganj, New Delhi 110002; soft cover; price ₹ 400.

The book has been written by a former professor of commerce at Delhi School of Economics, Universi-ty of Delhi. He was also vice-chancel-lor, University of North Bengal and consultant, School of Management Studies at Indira Gandhi National Open University.

First edition of the book was published way back in 1986. This is the fourteenth thoroughly revised and updated edition published this year.

Contents of the book are divided into nineteen sections with several subjects covered in each. It also includes many test questions and cases, plus university examination question papers. Index at the end of the book helps in locating subject matter.

The Indian context has been

kept in view throughout the book. The basic ideas presented are well supported by findings and studies relevant to India.

The book is written mainly for post-graduate students of manage-ment in Indian universities and institutes. The text has been put across in such a manner that Indian executives working in this field will also find it interesting and useful for reference.

The book begins with an over-view of strategic management pro-cess and goes on to strategic vision, corporate mission, objectives and goals in the second chapter. It ends with chapters on franchising and strategic management process: the case method.

MARKET SURVEY REPORTS

FACTS FOR YOU specialises in publishing market surveys. A large number of surveys have already been published. Some of these are:

Jan. 2013	Coir		Scheduled Commercial Banks
	Wheat		Life Insurance & Bancassurance
	Turmeric		
	Tamarind	**Nov. 2013**	Paper
	Tomatoes		Natural Honey
	Rural Tourism		Micro Insurance
			Khadi & Village Industries
Feb. 2013	Coal		
	Sugar	**Dec. 2013**	Unorganised Sectors
	Tourism		Small-Scale Industries
	Coconut Water		e-CRM Services of Banks
	Petroleum Products		
	Fast-Moving Consumer Goods	**Jan. 2014**	Cassava
			Sweet Potatoes
March 2013	Ports		Public-Private Partnerships
	Tyres		Food Processing Industries
	Commercial Paper		
	Fertiliser Industry	**Feb. 2014**	Salt
	Tourism in Gujarat		Toys
			Cabbage
April 2013	Guava		Cardamom
	Saffron		Civil Aviation
	Railways		
	Two-wheelers	**March 2014**	Gold
	India's Mobile Industry		Coconuts
			Cauliflower
May 2013	Tea		Smartphones
	Coal		SMEs in India
	Mentha		
	Wood Apple	**April 2014**	Onion
	Pomegranate		Gold Loan
	Tourism in Andhra Pradesh		Bitter Gourd
			Textile Industry
June 2013	Tobacco		Small-Scale Industries
	Services Sector		Green Energy Technologies
	Rural Telecommunications		
		May 2014	Cars
July 2013	Dairies		Stevia
	Tyre Industry		Tractors
	Gems & Jewellery		
	Tourism & Hotel Industry	**June 2014**	Jamun
			Banana
Aug. 2013	Gold		Cashew
	Cotton		Economic Development & IT
	Poultry		
	Saffron	**July 2014**	E-retailing
	Sugar Decontrol		Fertilisers
			Carrot
Sep. 2013	Tea		Advertising
	Rice		Insurance
	Turmeric		
	Edible Oils	**Aug. 2014**	Radish
	Custard Apple		Cement
Oct. 2013	Rubber		Aquaculture
	Rupee Depreciation		

For details contact:

Facts For You

D-87/1, Okhla Industrial Area, Phase-1, New Delhi 110020
Phone: 011-26810601/02/03; Fax: 26817563; E-mail: info@efy.in

STOCKS CLIMB IN CYCLICAL UPS AND DOWNS

July 2014 has been an exciting month for Indian investors. Stock prices rose and fell in periodic cycles, but the general trend continued to be upward. The BSE index stood at 25,516.35 on July 1, 2014. It climbed steadily and breached the 26,000 mark (26,100.08) within a week, on July 7. Predictions of a weak monsoon and consequent inflation did lead to a substantial fall in stock prices soon after, and the BSE fell to a low of 25,006.98 on July 14. But it soon bounced back, regained the 26,000 level, and stood at 26,271.85 on July 24. The last week of the month, however, again witnessed a slight dip in stock prices.

The NSE followed a similar trend. It stood at 7634.70 on July 1, climbed to 7787.15 on July 7, fell to 7454.15 on July 14, and was back at 7830.60 on July 24.

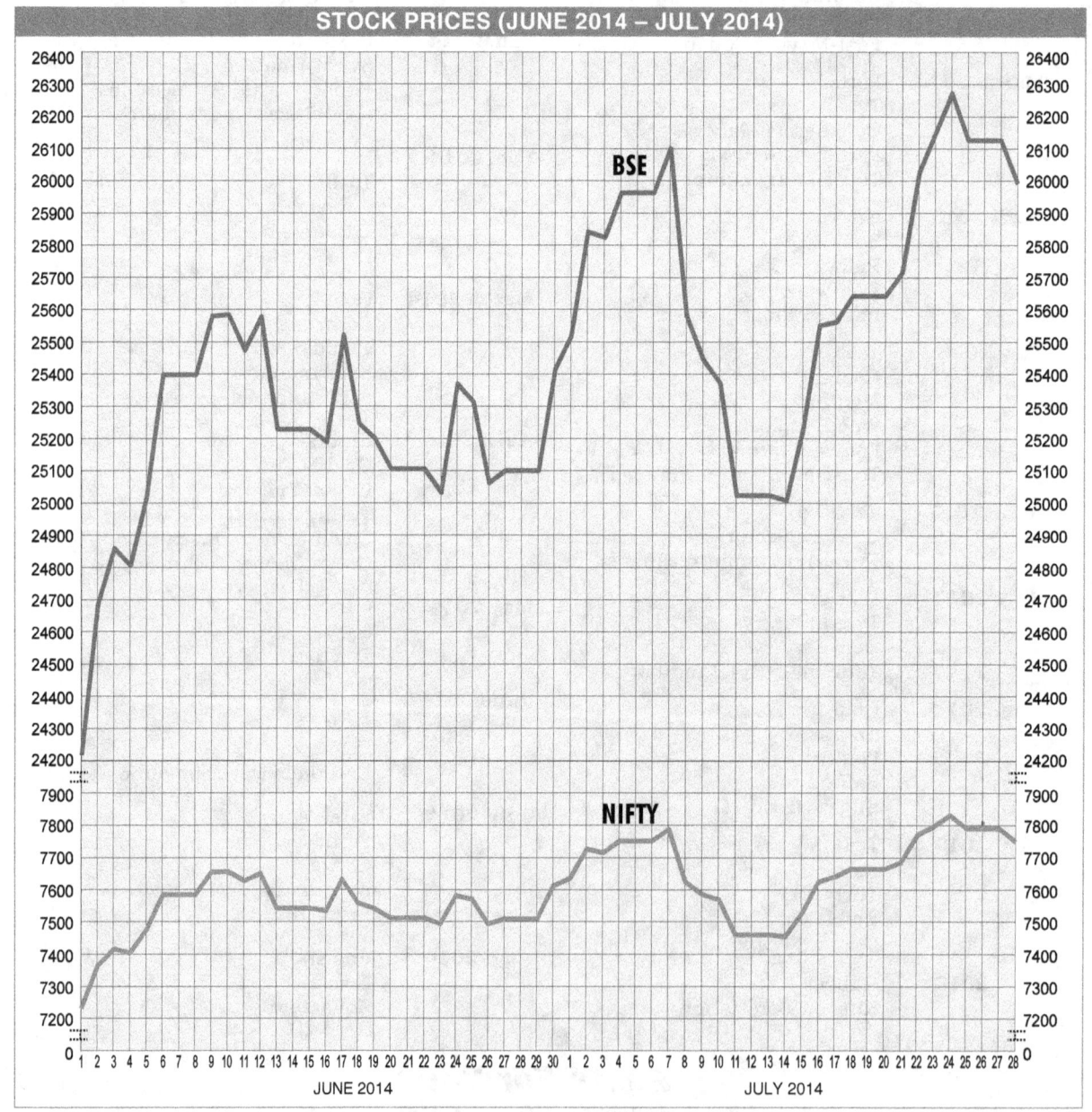

STOCK PRICES (JUNE 2014 – JULY 2014)

BSE

NIFTY

JUNE 2014   JULY 2014

R N I No.34506/79, Mailed on 3rd/4th of the month
Published on 3rd of the month

Delhi Postal Regd. No.DL(S)-01/3140/2012-14
Licenced to Post without Pre-Payment License No.U(SE)-27/2012-14